MW00583986

sauda␣e

saudade

an anthology
of fado poetry

Edited by **Mimi Khalvati**
Selected by **Vasco Graça Moura**

CALOUSTE
GULBENKIAN
FOUNDATION

Published by the
Calouste Gulbenkian Foundation
United Kingdom Branch
50 Hoxton Square
London N1 6PB
Tel: 020 7012 1400
Email: info@gulbenkian.org.uk
Website: www.gulbenkian.org.uk

Introduction © 2010 Mimi Khalvati
A Note on Fado History © 2010 Rui Vieira Nery
Poems commissioned for this anthology © 2010 Moniza Alvi, Judith
Barrington, David Constantine, Alfred Corn, Ruth Fainlight, Elaine Feinstein,
Grey Gowrie, Marilyn Hacker, Philip Jenkins, Fady Joudah, Sarah Maguire,
Eric Ormsby, Don Paterson, Pascale Petit, Carol Rumens, Fiona Sampson,
Michael Schmidt and George Szirtes

Copyright of the Portuguese poems remains with the poets or their estates.
The right of Mimi Khalvati to be identified as author of the Introduction and
editor of this work and of Rui Vieira Nery to be identified as author of the
Note on Fado History has been asserted in accordance with the Copyright,
Designs and Patents Act 1988.

ISBN 978 1 903080 13 9

British Library Cataloguing-in-Publication Data
A catalogue record for this book is available from the British Library

Designed by Helen Swansbourne
Printed by the MPG Books Group

Distributed by Central Books, 99 Wallis Road, London E9 5LN
Tel: 0845 458 9911, Fax: 0845 458 9912
Email: orders@centralbooks.com
Website: www.centralbooks.co.uk

Cover: Helena Almeida, *Inhabited Painting*, 1975. Acrylic on b&w
photograph. Size: 42 x 47.5 cm; 46 x 51.5 cm. Col. Banco Privado Português,
SA, at Fundação de Serralves – Museu de Arte Contemporânea, Porto.
Photograph © Laura Castro Caldas and Paulo Cintra.

CONTENTS

PREFACE

The idea for this collection of poems was sparked off in 2007 over a lunch with Lord Gowrie, critic, poet and former Arts Council Chairman. We were extolling the virtues of Portugal, headquarters of the Calouste Gulbenkian Foundation – its language, art, and music, and in particular of the unique musical tradition of Fado, which we both loved.

The music of Fado has become increasingly established internationally. However, outside Portugal, little is known about Fado's lyrical richness and complexity.

Saudade: An anthology of fado poetry, the first ever collection of Fado poems in English, is a unique venture which provides the English-reading public worldwide with access to the themes of Fado and a distinctive body of Portuguese literature. The anthology is a dual language publication that brings together 53 original Fado poems, and their newly created English 'versions', which range in approach from almost literal translations to loose 'imitations' – imaginative tributes inspired by the originals. Translated literature has great potential for enabling inter-cultural dialogue and an increased understanding between people from different cultural backgrounds – one of the main aims of the UK Branch in our work to enrich and connect the lives of individuals.

The Fado poets and poems featured were selected by distinguished Portuguese poet Vasco Graça Moura, an expert in the field who is himself an award-winning translator into Portuguese and whose work has been translated into several languages. London-based, Tehran-born poet Mimi Khalvati, whose work has also been widely translated and whose poetic interests lie in the affiliations between poetry and song, was appointed editor, becoming responsible for the selection of 18 of the finest contemporary poets writing in English. These were chosen both for their abilities as poets and for the breadth of their experience and knowledge of translating from a range of languages.

Sourcing the Fado poems as originally created by their authors was a considerable challenge. Some of the poems were never published or registered in any form by their creators and Fado singers often alter lyrics according to their own preference or understanding, so it is almost impossible to be sure which version to use. In some cases the lyrics were extremely difficult to find in a reliable printed version which meant that some of the poems featured in this publication had to be captured by listening to (often old) recordings, leaving great margins for error. *Saudade* was never intended to be a definitive collection of Fado poetry, but all efforts have been made to present the poems in their correct, original versions and apologies are offered for any inaccuracies.

The Portuguese originals were carefully selected to include a wide range of Fado poems – old and new, traditional and erudite, romantic and political – in order to provide a comprehensive picture of a genre that celebrates love and longing, but simultaneously reflects the complexities of Portuguese history and culture over the past two centuries. The Foundation provided a range of opportunities to familiarise the poets with every aspect of Fado, but they were then free to create new versions in their own style. *Saudade* has become a work about translation itself, a reflection on the possibilities and limitations posed by a juxtaposition of cultures and an exploration of the range of solutions available to overcome cultural barriers.

I should like to express my gratitude to the many individuals and institutions without whose knowledge and dedicated efforts this publication would not have been possible: to Grey Gowrie for inspiring the idea, to Mimi Khalvati who has edited the anthology with exemplary care and style, to Rui Nery for his authoritative note on Fado's history, to my colleagues Louisa Hooper and Isabel Lucena, to designer Helen Swansbourne and most especially to the poets whose new works appear here. In addition a lot of invaluable background information has been provided by many Portuguese people deeply involved with the living tradition of Fado – *muito obrigado*!

Andrew Barnett
UK Branch Director
Calouste Gulbenkian Foundation
April 2010

A NOTE ON FADO HISTORY

Fado is a genre of urban popular song which developed in Lisbon from the mid nineteenth century. Its most direct antecedent was an African-Brazilian genre of sung dance with the same name, widely practised at the beginning of the century in the most important cities of Brazil, then still part of the Portuguese empire. This dance, described by several European travellers of the time as both sensual and sentimental, seems to have first arrived in Lisbon in the early 1820s, when the return of the Portuguese royal family from exile in Rio de Janeiro (1821) and the declaration of Brazilian independence (1822) resulted in a significant flow of immigration from the former colony to Portugal. Together with the returning dignitaries of the court and the colonial administration, a crowd of tradesmen, sailors, servants and slaves arrived in Lisbon and established themselves mostly in the lower-class neighbourhoods close to the city harbour, and their songs and dances soon integrated with the cultural practices of the local population. The dance component of the genre, often designated as 'bater o Fado' ('to beat the Fado'), remained in use almost until the end of the nineteenth century, although the purely musical aspect quickly gained a wider popularity.

The original patterns of this colonial Fado soon mingled with characteristics of the local popular song traditions from Lisbon itself and other regions of the country, as the capital now attracted large contingents of immigrants fleeing from the aftermath of the Napoleonic invasions (1807–15) and the Portuguese civil wars (1828–34). This early process of fusion is nevertheless difficult to establish in great detail, given the lack of notated sources until the 1850s. At the beginning of its development in Lisbon, Fado was located mostly in venues of popular entertainment, such as taverns and brothels, in the poorest areas of the city. It soon attracted, however, the curiosity of the bohemian youth of the upper middle class and the aristocracy. A young prostitute from the red light district of Mouraria, Maria Severa Onofriana (1820–46), famous for her gifts as a Fado singer and for being the mistress of the Count of Vimioso, was to become the first icon in the history of the genre.

The interest in Fado amongst the middle classes of Lisbon grew steadily. From the mid nineteenth century Fado melodies began to be published as sheet music for voice and piano or piano solo, becoming part of the salon repertoire of the time, alongside the best known excerpts from French operetta and Italian opera. In 1873 the first public concert of Fado took place in the prestigious Lisbon Casino, and soon the genre was adopted as a mainstay of the music theatre, even though at first it was performed by comedy artists rather than by the Fado singers themselves. With the growth of the Portuguese labour and socialist movement in the 1870s, Fado was often used as a means of political and ideological propaganda, and many well-known Fado singers took part in political rallies organised in Lisbon and the main industrial regions of the country. Lyrics of this 'Fado operário' ('workers' Fado') often refer to the fundamentals of the revolutionary credo and pay homage to such key figures of the international socialist and anarchist movement as Marx, Engels, Bakunin and Kropotkin. This strong left-wing trend did not, however, prevent the popularity of the genre spreading through the whole spectrum of Lisbon society, transcending all ideological or political barriers. The beginnings of the gramophone industry in Portugal around 1902 led to numerous recordings by the best-known Fado singers and so greatly contributed to its dissemination.

During the First Portuguese Republic (1910–26) this expansion was strengthened by the increasing number of restaurants and beer houses which now hired Fado singers to perform on a regular basis for their customers, usually catering to a middle class audience attracted by the management's assurance of the utter respectability of its clientele. In this way, important performers like António Lado, António Pedro Machado ('Machadinho'), António Rosa ('Rosa Sapateiro'), António Santos ('Ginguinha') and Francisco Viana ('Vianinha') gained a new professional status in the country's cultural industry.

The extreme right wing coup d'état of 1926 led to a military dictatorship which immediately established the censorship of the press and of public entertainment. In 1927 new legislation imposed strict safety rules for all entertainment businesses, but also demanded that artists carry an official 'professional card' and that the lyrics of their repertory be authorised by the censorship board. All poetical subjects connected with the 'Fado operário' tradition or in any way considered offensive to the state or the Catholic Church were strictly forbidden. In the early 1930s the birth of radio broadcasting in Portugal and the growth of the record industry were powerful vehicles for the promotion of the genre on a national scale.

Clubs and restaurants known as 'casas de Fado' ('Fado houses'), offering nightly programmes of Fado with a resident artistic staff, opened throughout the older neighbourhoods of the city. The 'Salão Artístico de Fados' (1927), the 'Solar da Alegria' (1928), the 'Café Luso' (1931), the 'Retiro da Severa' (1933), the 'Adega Mesquita' (1938) and the 'Adega Machado' (1939) attracted a strong middle class clientele and further encouraged the professionalisation of Fado singers. Amongst the most famous of these were Berta Cardoso, Ercília Costa, Ermelinda Vitória, Madalena de Melo, Maria do Carmo Torres, Alberto Costa, Alfredo Duarte ('Marceneiro'), Joaquim Campos and Filipe Pinto. The performance routine of the Fado houses as well as the technical demands of the record industry and of radio broadcasting strongly influenced and standardised the performance style of the genre, defining the rules that are now regarded as its core tradition in the twentieth century. The standard duration of a Fado is three to four minutes, thus fitting on one side of a 78rpm record. A characteristic performance involves a solo singer, male or female, and instrumental accompaniment by a Portuguese guitar (a pear-shaped, twelve-string metal-strung instrument of the cittern family) and a six-string metal-strung Spanish guitar. From the 1950s this accompaniment was often expanded to two Portuguese guitars, a Spanish guitar and an acoustic bass guitar.

In the 1930s and 40s Fado also remained a strong element in the theatrical life of Lisbon, with some of the best Fado singers, such as Ercília Costa or Hermínia Silva, often hired as guest artists within the casts of the popular 'revistas' (traditional Portuguese vaudeville). The theatre connection led to the adoption of a new formal pattern in the composition of Fados known as 'Fado canção' ('Fado song'), based on an alternation of refrain and couplets, which coexisted with the more traditional strophic forms that remained as the basis of the Fado repertoire.

Although the military dictatorship of 1926 soon evolved into an authoritarian regime strongly influenced by Italian Fascism, the state did not try to produce any kind of officially sponsored aesthetic ideology in the field of popular music. Since political criticism was safely excluded by censorship, the regime unofficially encouraged authors to handle topics related to the historical achievements of the Portuguese, especially the great maritime voyages of the sixteenth century, the glorification of the country's colonial empire or traditional religious subjects. It mostly favoured 'apolitical', sentimental themes of a sad, fatalistic nature, jealousy, amorous infidelity, loneliness or longing for lost happiness. For the official institutions of the regime, however, Fado was too lower class, too urban and too recent to be considered part of the true Portuguese cultural identity, the preference being for older rural genres officially promoted as 'folklore'.

The post World War II era, with the defeat of the fascist regimes and the victory of Western democracies, forced the Portuguese state to abandon many of the external signs of its totalitarian roots. The regime now sought to present itself as a populist authoritarian system, with a benevolent rule close to the traditional values of the Portuguese people. The official attitude towards Fado thus changed gradually, with the government now trying to cash in on the genre's immense popularity. Fado began to be included in official cultural events, as well as in the programming of the state-owned radio network, the Emissora Nacional, and in the so-called 'Serões para Trabalhadores' ('workers' evenings') promoted by the Fundação Nacional para a Alegria no Trabalho ('National Foundation for Joy at Work'). The newly established state television (1957) and the film industry also granted Fado a significant role, usually presenting it as the Portuguese 'national song'.

The growth of the tourist industry in the 1950s and 60s turned Fado into a key attraction for foreign visitors. Fado houses now often dubbed themselves as 'casas típicas' ('typical houses') and many new establishments opened during this period, each usually with a resident artistic cast centered around a well-known singer: Adelina Ramos in A Tipóia, Fernanda Maria in Lisboa à Noite, Carlos Ramos in A Toca, Argentina Santos in A Parreirinha de Alfama, Lucília do Carmo in A Adega da Lucília and Fernando Farinha in Adega Mesquita, amongst others. Outside this professional circuit the Countess of Sabrosa, Maria Teresa de Noronha, also had an important career. The Countess came from an aristocratic circle in which amateur Fado singing had been a family tradition and she became famous through her regular radio broadcasts on Emissora Nacional and her numerous recordings.

Amália Rodrigues was another exceptional case. She rose to unmatched national stardom throughout the 1940s and then proceeded to build a unique international career in the following four decades. From the very beginning, Amália sang not only the lyrics written by a lineage of popular poets rooted in the tradition of Fado (Linhares Barbosa, Frederico de Brito) but also poems by erudite authors such David Mourão-Ferreira, Pedro Homem de

Mello and Sidónio Muralha. This trend was even more pronounced from 1961 when she started an important artistic partnership with composer Alain Oulman, who wrote numerous Fados for her in a new style, not only resorting to harmonic and formal innovations until then foreign to the Fado tradition but also setting lyrics by some of the greatest Portuguese poets. These were both contemporary – Mourão-Ferreira and Homem de Mello, and also, for example Alexandre O'Neil, Manuel Alegre and José Carlos Ary dos Santos – and classical – including Portugal's national poet from the sixteenth century, Luis de Camões, an association seen by conservatives as little less than scandalous. From the early 1970s a second Fado performer, this time male, Carlos do Carmo, also built a significant international career, and contributed as well to an aesthetic renewal of the genre.

With the democratic revolution on 25 April 1974 the popularity of Fado suffered a severe blow. Accused of being a docile vehicle for the ideology of the fallen dictatorship, initially the genre was practically banished from radio and television by the new radical administrations. There seemed to be very few Fado performers among the younger generation, and it was widely believed that its very survival was at stake, beyond the few artists whose careers were already safely launched (João Braga, Maria da Fé, Rodrigo, Teresa Tarouca, Carlos Zel, Beatriz da Conceição). Its popularity, however, never really diminished, and from the early 1980s a new generation of performers began to emerge. Some did not consider themselves to be Fado singers per se, although they might adopt part of the repertory of Amália and often used a vocal technique similar to that of Fado (Teresa Salgueiro, Dulce Pontes). Some experimented with crossovers between Fado and other popular music genres such as pop rock or even punk (António Variações, Paulo Bragança). Others emerged mostly from outside Portugal and the traditions of the original Fado circles, and enjoyed very successful careers within World Music circuits (Mísia, Cristina Branco). The majority, nevertheless, could be placed in the mainstream of the genre, combining in various degrees fidelity to the more traditional strophic Fados of the first half of the century and an expansion of the repertory with new composers, new poets, and new arrangements. These were often influenced by jazz, for example in the replacement of the bass guitar by the double bass. Among the latter are Camané, Mafalda Arnauth, Katia Guerreiro, Ana Sofia Varela, Ricardo Ribeiro and Carmo Rebelo de Andrade

('Carminho'). A special mention must be made of Mariza, whose international stardom has now reached the highest level of the world entertainment industry (Edisonpreis, BBC Artist of the Year, Grammy Nomination for Best Latin Artist).

The last two decades also saw increasing interest in the study and preservation of the Fado tradition. After an important exhibition dedicated to the genre within the programme of Lisbon 94, European Cultural Capital (*Vozes e Sombras*, directed by anthropologist Joaquim Pais de Brito), a Museum of Fado was established by the Lisbon City Council in 1998. The Ethnomusicology Institute of the Universidade Nova de Lisboa, headed by Salwa Castelo-Branco, is leading a research project in this field, including an inventory of sound recordings, iconography and musical editions, as well as interviews with leading exponents of the genre. An application for Fado to be recognised by UNESCO as an 'Intangible Cultural Heritage of Humanity' is currently being prepared under the patronage of the Lisbon City Council.

Rui Vieira Nery
Instituto de Etnomusicologia
Centro de Estudos de Música e Dança

INTRODUCTION

Longing, yearning, nostalgia, homesickness, a feeling akin to the Welsh *hiraeth* or the German *Heimweh*, *saudade* is traditionally associated with sailors homesick for land. But listening to Isabel Lucena at the Calouste Gulbenkian Foundation explain, I had my first real inkling of its sensation when she pointed out that 'longing' reaches outwards, looks beyond horizons, whereas *saudade* – and here she clasped her hands close to her heart – is holding the object of your longing close to you, cherishing it, drawing it ever deeper inwards.

Saudade, the 'longing' which lies at the heart of Fado, here signals the first time an anthology of Fado poems has been assembled. No such anthology has appeared either in the original Portuguese or in English translation. But Fado songs are known and loved worldwide and we hope that, by providing the lyrics around which Fado songs are created, an essential and hitherto missing element will be available to aficionados as well as to those new to Fado. We also hope they will appeal to poetry lovers and those interested in translation.

To have been invited by the Gulbenkian Foundation to edit this anthology was an honour and a daunting responsibility. I knew nothing of Fado, only a few words of Portuguese and little more about Portuguese culture than I'd learned in the 60s living for a year in the village of Alte. Rather irrelevantly, the first line of a folk song came back to me: *Não pode ser. Não pode, não* ('It cannot be. Oh no, it cannot')... along with its accompanying gesture, a wagging finger, and the rest of the tune tapping its way through my body. However, it was reassuring to know that the Gulbenkian placed value on the process – artists discovering something entirely new to them – as well as on the final publication, and that this would hold true for the poets invited to translate the Fado lyrics as well as for me.

Our eighteen Anglophone poet-translators need little introduction to poetry readers. Distinguished poets in their own right, renowned in their concomitant roles as publishers, editors, critics, many are also among our most celebrated translators into English. Between them they have translated from a wealth of languages: German, Russian, Hungarian, Estonian, Arabic, Somali, Dari, Chinese, Korean, Nahuatl

(Aztec), as well as from the main Romance languages including Portuguese. Modern Poetry in Translation and The Poetry Translation Centre, two of our landmark organisations, are spearheaded by David Constantine and Sarah Maguire respectively. Michael Schmidt, as editor of Carcanet Press, has a long-established, prized list of notable translations, including *Contemporary Portuguese Poetry* (1978), the first anthology of its kind published in Britain.

As translators, our poets fall into two groups: those who are bilingual or have other languages at their command and translate directly from original works, and those who work with the aid of literal transcriptions, prose cribs, alternative translations, or in collaboration with the authors of source texts. In translating these 53 Fado poems, both contemporary and traditional, contributors were provided with literal translations, spoken and sung recordings of their Fado poems, a glossary, a history of Fado and above all, the expertise of Isabel Lucena, who offered an invaluable reference point for elucidation and discussion. Where possible, our translators were given Portuguese poems by the same author and the chance to inhabit a single voice. Many of them have highlighted how listening to the sung recordings was the channel through which they began to 'hear' the poem and to find the melody of their English versions.

During the editing of *Saudade*, I was offered a weekend in Lisbon: a glorious chance to hear Fado in its natural setting, guided by Helder Moutinho, himself a Fado singer and brother of the famous Camané. I had only seen Lisbon once, en route back to England from Alte. But here were the cobbled streets where fishwives used to hawk their wares; crumbling plaster walls, drying laundry, arches above steep winding steps with their promise of a vista; doors through which Severa, the first great Fado singer, might have stooped to enter her ramshackle dwelling. Here was the commercial quarter, Chiado, and the café 'A Brasileira' where revolutionaries used to meet at tables so old that the chipped corners had been cut off, leaving oddly-shaped tabletops and, outside the café, a statue of Pessoa, in hat and bowtie, conversing with an empty chair. And here, in Bairro Alto, was the tiny tavern Tasca do Xico, too crowded for us to do more than peer in through the open windows, just as Mariza peered into her father's tavern as a child, before asking him 'Can I sing Fado?'

At last, we did hear Fado: at the elegant restaurant 'Clube de Fado' in Alfama where its owner Mario Pacheco, accompanist and composer for the great Amália, performed on Portuguese guitar, accompanying Miguel Capucho and Joana Amendoeira (whose name means 'almond tree'); at 'Senhor Vinho' in the Madragoa district, where Mariza and singers of the new Fado generation launched their careers and where we heard António Zambujo blending Fado with Cante, from his native Alentjo, and Brazilian rhythms.

Whether grand or humble, the Fado houses held the same electric atmosphere. Dimmed lights, obligatory silence, forbidden entry mid-performance, created an expectancy, a tension both theatrical and reverent. Melismatic vocals, wringing ropes of sound miraculously sustained are familiar to me from Persian classical music. But I was not prepared for the intimacy, the dynamic range, particularly in the softer registers, nor for the acute sense of dialogue – in the dramatic sense of protagonists 'playing an action': pleading, cajoling, rejecting, seducing, reaching and retracting outwards and inwards. Fado seems to be less about the beauty of the voice than the depth of the soul, but it's difficult to venture anything about its spirit without sounding corny or falling foul of cultural diffidence. Indeed many Fado songs are about Fado itself, as hard to define as *saudade*, which, the Portuguese will tell you, 'is impossible to translate'.

Without body, voice, gesture, are Fado songs impossible to translate? Yet some were texts before they were songs: popular rhymes sometimes randomly assembled; then later, 'real' poems from some of Portugal's finest poets, such as David Mourão-Ferreira, Pedro Homem de Mello and Alexandre O'Neill, or lyrics composed for the *fadistas* who then started to write their own. The spirit of improvisation, *desgerrada*, is also important to Fado, just as the singers, styling and interpreting the fixed tunes, establish their own distinctive claims. By extension, our poets, through the act of translation, carry on this tradition of interpretation, embellishment, improvisation.

Of course, translation involves not only rendering a text, but also negotiating between two cultures. Arguments about the respective merits of foreignisation and domestication are endemic and call into question our ethical and aesthetic values. Poetry itself is estranging and translation, when it defamiliarises by allowing the 'foreign' to have a palpable presence in the text, further makes it new. But does this sacrifice intelligibility, readability? Poetry often asks for the subjugation of ego and translation for the ceding of one voice to another. But can this result in a true poem without the necessary connection to the writer's self and experience? Our translators have faced not only the dilemmas that come with any translation, but those of poems designed to be *sung*, and moreover emblematic of a national identity. Generously, in their notes, they identify some of the particular challenges.

Form is intrinsic to Fado poems: stanzaic forms, quatrains, metre, rhyme. And here prosodic arguments come into play: by adhering to formal strictures, does one lose fidelity to meaning? Is meaning primarily semantic, or also musical, sub-surface, symbolic in its formal tenets? Will metre require padding, given that languages have different kinds of elasticity, taking a longer or shorter time to travel the same distance? Will the loss of rhyme entail a loss of acoustic intensity? The questions are endless. And then there is the minefield of cultural aesthetics. Simplicity in one language may be banality in another, sweetness in one sentimental in the next. I remember being asked, while translating a poem from Urdu and querying a syntactical ambiguity: 'Why is English so *logical?*'

But our brave translators are also ingenious. They have looked for assistance to other lyrical forms, such as the ballad, French chanson, Hungarian pop songs, Elizabethan verse, the mawaal and the ghazal. They have ranged along the spectrum from literal translation, through versions, to the time-honoured tradition of *hommage* in imitations – think Lorca, Pound, Lowell. Occasionally, they have transposed gender as the singers often do or left words, place names, titles, in the original Portuguese. But above all, they have sought to translate the relationship between Fado and its audience: that of love, which has connected so naturally with their own love of the songs and for which they have found new words.

At every stage of this book, Isabel Lucena and Louisa Hooper have been a source of invaluable help. Particular thanks are also due to Andrew Barnett for the original idea, Rui Nery for his essay on Fado and early advice, Vasco Graça Moura for selecting the Portuguese poems, Ana Cristina Louro for providing the literal translations, Liliana Costa (Liana) for recording the spoken poems and Helen Swansbourne for the design. I am deeply grateful to the Calouste Gulbenkian Foundation for the hospitality that translation always affords, and more, for this opportunity to enjoy pleasures from Portuguese culture that so richly enhance our own.

Mimi Khalvati

saudade

MONIZA ALVI

Translating the Fado poems was indeed a challenge, in terms of their specific cultural references, as well as their style. My aim was to be faithful to the ambience of the originals while producing natural-sounding, song-like poems in English. The more I found out about the cultural and political background of the poems, the history of Fado, and of Roman Catholicism in Portugal, the more I felt it essential to reflect this background in the translations, rather than to make versions that might be more expected by a British reader. The enjoyment of the task became the possibility of bringing a very different tradition into view. While retaining the short, essentially simple lines and the song-like, I didn't want to lose the passion of Fado.

'Podes Dizer que Sou Teu' ('Maria, I Am Yours') appeared the lighter of my three poems, and this was born out when I heard it sung. Correspondingly, full, if irregular rhymes seemed appropriate. It was useful to learn more about the origins of the traditional headscarf, the rustic aspects of Fado's roots, along with Fado's connection with prayer. 'O Pierrot' ('The Pierrot') is strikingly beautiful when sung, and the challenge was to keep to the songlike without lightening this sorrowful poem, so I tended to make use of half-rhymes. In 'Lembro-me de Ti' ('I Remember You') it was helpful to learn that cigarette smoking at the time the poem would have been written (pre-1965) was a sign of sophistication, rather than of 'low living', and that not many women smoked. In this poem I reduced the number of lines in each stanza to produce a distilled version in English, and separated off the 'I remember you' to increase, in translation, the singing effect.

JOÃO LINHARES BARBOSA

Lembro-me de Ti

Eu Lembro-me de ti
Chamavas-te Saudade
Vivias num moinho
Ao cimo do outeiro
Tamanquinha no pé,
Lenço posto à vontade
Nesse tempo eras tu,
A filha do Moleiro

Eu lembro-me de ti,
Passavas para a fonte
Pousando no quadril
O cântaro de barro
Imitavas em graça
A cotovia insonte
E mungias o gado
Até encher o tarro

Eu lembro-me de ti,
E às vezes a farinha
Vestia-te de branco,
E parecias-me então
Uma Virgem gentil
Que fosse à capelinha
Num dia de manhã
Fazer a Comunhão

Eu lembro-me de ti,
E fico-me aturdido
Ao ver-te pela rua
Em gargalhadas francas
Pretendo confundir
A pele do teu vestido
Com a sedosa lã
Das ovelhinhas brancas

Eu lembro-me de ti,
Ao ver-te no casino
Descarada a fumar
Luxuoso cigarro
Fecho os olhos e vejo
O teu busto franzino
Com o avental da cor
Do cântaro de barro

Eu lembro-me de ti,
Quando no torvelinho
Da dança sensual
Passas louca rolando
Eu sonho, eu fantasio
E vejo o teu moinho
Que bailava também
Ao vento assobiando

Eu Lembro-me de ti,
E fico-me a cismar
Que o nome de Luci,
Que tens não é verdade
Que saudade que eu tenho,
E leio no teu olhar
A saudade que tens
De quando eras Saudade

I Remember You

I remember you

when you were Saudade,
with your flowing scarf,
and your wooden shoes,
you lived in the windmill
on top of the hill, Saudade,
the miller's daughter

I remember you

an innocent girl
graceful as the skylark,
off to the fountain,
a clay pitcher on your hip,
or milking the cows
with a brimming pail

I remember you

the times when the flour
cloaked you in white,
and you walked to the chapel
for Holy Communion,
a gentle Virgin Mary,
that's how you seemed to me

I remember you

and now I'm shocked to see
you're so bold, so brazen,
laughing loudly in the street
and I change the skin
of your tight silk dress
to a soft lamb's fleece

I remember you

girl at the casino, shameless,
smoking an expensive cigarette –
but I close my eyes
and glimpse your apron,
brown as a clay pitcher,
your delicate breast

I remember you

your provocative dance
the whirling and reeling,
and I can't help dreaming
dreaming of the mill sails
whirling as they did
in the whistling wind

I remember you

and I can't stop thinking
that Luci's not your name,
I have so much longing
so much *saudade,*
and I see *saudade* in your eyes,
a longing for the old Saudade

JOÃO LINHARES BARBOSA

Podes Dizer que Sou Teu

Maria, na quinta-feira
Põe teu xaile de merino
Como queres ser cantadeira
Segue lá o teu destino
E vive à tua maneira

Mas toma muito cuidado
Porque o fado tem seus quês
Canta de xaile traçado
Põe um lenço português
Porque assim é que é o fado

Há quem te vá censurar
Por cantares de xaile e lenço
Mas deixa o mundo falar
Pois se ele pensar como eu penso
De certo se há-de calar

O lenço é gentil brazão
Que a tradição nos cedeu
E se o fado é oração
Nao é de cabeça ao léu
Que se faz a confissão

A Mouraria morreu
Ficas tu para a recordar
Com um lenço bem plebeu
E um xaile de agasalhar
Podes dizer que sou teu

Maria, I Am Yours

So you wish to wear a shawl
of fine merino wool –
wear it on Thursday
and sing, transfix us all.
Live as you must, live as you will.

But Maria, there are 'buts',
Maria, take good care,
wear a shawl across your shoulders
but a headscarf for your hair
because that's how *fado* is.

Let the world grumble, let it laugh
and mock your singing
in a shawl and scarf.
If people feel as I do,
in the end they'll stop.

Remember, *fado's* a kind of prayer –
you'd never make confession
with your head bare.
So be grateful for the scarf,
it's *fado's* gift to you.

Old customs are dying out,
but they'll stay alive in you.
Maria, I am yours
with your humble scarf
and your warm merino shawl.

JOÃO LINHARES BARBOSA

O Pierrot

Naquele dia de entrudo, lembro bem
Um intrigante Pierrot, da cor do céu
Um ramo de violetas, pequeninas
À linda morta atirou, como um adeus

Passa triste o funeral, é duma virgem
Mas ao povo que lhe importa, aquele enterro
Que a morte lhe passa à porta, só por ele
Em dia de carnaval, e de vertigem

Abaixo a máscara gritei, com energia
Quem és tu grosseiro que ousas, profanar
Perturbar a paz das lousas, tumulares
E o Pierrot disse não sei, que não sabia

Sei apenas que a adorei, um certo dia
Num amor todo grilhetas, assassinas
Se não vim de vestes pretas, em ruínas
Visto de negro o coração, e resoluto

Atirou sobre o caixão, como um tributo
Um ramo de violetas, pequeninas
Atirou sobre o caixão, como um tributo
Um ramo de violetas, pequeninas

The Pierrot

I recall so well on carnival day
a small bunch of violets, a heavenly blue,
the pierrot who threw them to say goodbye
to a beautiful girl who was buried that day.

The saddest funeral of a sacred girl
on that dizzy, joyous carnival day –
and could the townspeople really care
at another death passing by the door?

Pierrot, I yelled: Take off your mask!
Who are you to come dressed like this?
It's an insult to her, to the peace of the dead.
But I loved her, adored her, he said.

Loved her madly to this day,
bound by a love that was destroying me.
Hidden beneath these pierrot's clothes
my sorrowing heart wears black.

He made his tribute, who could stop him?
Faithfully he made his tribute,
threw the violets over her coffin.
Violets – the very smallest bunch.

MICHAEL SCHMIDT

To transpose a poem whose natural element is music and voice into mere text is hard. Transposing into the largely monosyllabic registers of English songs that are so richly polysyllabic and vocalic in the Portuguese is also hard. There are no equivalences. The tentative syntax of the Portuguese calls out for a loosening of syntax in English. (I borrow the 'gapping' technique Elaine Feinstein devised for her Tsvetaeva translations, though her motives there are to render individual voice.) When, additionally, the poems attach themselves to specific places, with no English twinned towns or neighbourhoods, the translator is stymied. Should one draw a metaphor out of the place name, or leave the original in order to point the poem at its home?

I have translated complex poetry – by José López Velarde, by Octavio Paz and Pasternak and Hofmannsthal; I have translated, obliquely, from the Nahuatl (Aztec). No translation has been as challenging as this. I wanted to find a popular form, but I could not find enough in the original to flesh out a ballad. The narrative in the Fado poems is patent, taken for granted. The songs and their conventions are so second nature to the Portuguese imagination that the translator's questions hardly make sense to the native auditor.

I have heard many Fado singers in Lisbon, and I fall under the spell of this art because of its sufficiency, the totality of the form, its utter difference from any English or even Spanish form I know. Should I have attempted what Leonard Cohen does with Lorca in 'Take This Waltz', performing with a kind of heightened fidelity? But Cohen has the advantage of music and of a very fleshed out original. I thought of the songs of Chavela Vargas, but in them too the narrative is much more foregrounded, there is manifest, not inherent drama.

My conclusion after working on these extremely simple, extremely difficult poems, is that *saudade* is an inherence; like Geist, as soon as you try to extrapolate it, the energy passes out of it and it falls dead to the ground: 'all I ever meant/and what I can't define.' These songs are delicate and in my English versions all I try to do is not to damage them too much. English is not a hospitable element for them, and readers should become auditors and seek out the music and the Portuguese.

ANÍBAL NAZARÉ

Tudo Isto é Fado

Perguntaste-me outro dia
Se eu sabia o que era o fado
Eu disse que não sabia
Tu ficaste admirado
Sem saber o que dizia
Eu menti naquela hora
E disse que não sabia
Mas vou-te dizer agora

Almas vencidas,
Noites perdidas,
Sombras bizarras
Na Mouraria,
Canta um rufia,
Choram guitarras
Amor ciúme,
Cinzas e lume
Dor e pecado
Tudo isto existe
Tudo isto é triste
Tudo isto é fado

Se queres ser meu senhor
E teres-me sempre a teu lado
Não me fales só de amor
Fala-me também do fado
É canção que é meu castigo
Só nasceu p'ra me perder
O fado é tudo o que eu digo
Mais o que eu não sei dizer

All This is Fado

The other day you asked
Do you know what fado is
I've no idea I said
You looked at me amazed
Not knowing what I meant
I lied that hour to you
And said I'd no idea
But now I'm going to say

Lost souls   night-wasted hours
Shadows that haunt
In Mouraria a thug sings   guitars
Cry love and jealousy   firelight
And ash   Pain's there   sin too
All this indeed exists
All this is real sadness
And all of this is fado

If you want to master me
And keep me close by you
Don't talk of love only
Talk about fado too
The song's my punishment
Was born to do me in
Oh fado   all I ever meant
And what I can't define

ANÍBAL NAZARÉ

O Fado Mora em Lisboa

Passeia, p'lo mundo inteiro
Por gostar da vida boa
Mas não mora no estrangeiro
O fado mora em Lisboa.

Já morou na Mouraria,
Mas depois num sobressalto
Tratou da mudança e um dia
Foi p'ro Bairro Alto.

O fadinho mora sempre, por castigo,
Num bairro antigo, num bairro antigo,
E a seu lado, p'ra falarem à vontade
Mora a saudade, mora a saudade.

Quase em frente, numa casa de pobreza
Vive a tristeza, vive a tristeza,
Tem corrido os velhos bairros sempre à toa
Mas mora em Lisboa, mas mora em Lisboa.

Quando vai cantar lá fora
Tem uma ideia bizarra.
Leva um estribilho que chora
Na voz triste da guitarra.

Canta lá dias a fio
Mas, depois numa ansiedade,
Volta sempre num navio
Chamado Saudade.

O fadinho mora sempre, por castigo,
Num bairro antigo, num bairro antigo,
E a seu lado, p'ra falarem à vontade
Mora a saudade, mora a saudade.

Quase em frente, numa casa de pobreza
Vive a tristeza, vive a tristeza,
Tem corrido os velhos bairros sempre à toa
Mas mora em Lisboa, mas mora em Lisboa.

Quase em frente, numa casa de pobreza
Vive a tristeza, vive a tristeza,
Tem corrido os velhos bairros sempre à toa
Mas mora em Lisboa, mas mora em Lisboa.

Fado Belongs in Lisbon

Round the world it roams
Trying the good life out
It doesn't stay   it's back
Lisbon's fado's home

It lingers in Mouraria
For a while   then makes a move
In one day attempting
The climb to Bairro Alto

But fado's doomed to staying
In alleys   in the slums
Beside it   (so they can whisper)
Goes yearning   heart yearning

Across the way   a cheerless place
Where sadness   sadness lives
Fado's cruised each *barrio* slum
But Lisbon   Lisbon's its space.

When it leaves home to go singing
It has a wild intent
It utters a shrill refrain
To the guitar's lament

Day after day it sings
Then anxiously returns
Home as in a sailing ship
With Yearning on the stern.

Fado's doomed to staying
In alleys   in the slums
Beside it   (so they can whisper)
Goes yearning   heart yearning

Across the way   a cheerless place
Where sadness   sadness lives
Fado's cruised each *barrio* slum
But Lisbon   Lisbon's its space.

Across the way   a cheerless place
Where sadness   sadness lives
Fado's cruised each *barrio* slum
But Lisbon   Lisbon's its space.

ALBERTO RODRIGUES

Reviver o Passado

Fui à procura do fado
P'ra saber onde vivia
Corri toda a Lisboa
Procurei por todo o lado
Fui à velha Mouraria
Bairro Alto e Madragoa

Por toda a parte escutei
Viras sambas e canções
Num gosto mal prevertido
Confesso então que chorei
Que julguei por tais razões
Que o fado tinha morrido

Foi então que fui a Alfama
A esta velhinha terna
E quem cá encontrei por fim
O fado que a enflama
Dentro da tosca taberna
Uma voz cantava assim

Minha guitarra velhinha
O teu constante gemer
A minha tortura acalma
És parte da vida minha
Tornas mais leve o sofrer
Suavizas minha alma

E quando um dia partir
De vez para a eternidade
Recorda meus tristes ais
Como não te posso ouvir
Não sentir saudade
Guitarra não toques mais

To Relive the Past

I went in search of fado
To find out where it lived
I did the rounds of Lisbon
I questioned every shadow
In Mouraria   in Bairro
Alto and Madragoa

Each place I went I heard
Corrupted by bad taste
Repeated sambas   trite songs
I confess   I cried
Thinking because of these
Fado itself had died

I ended up in Alfama
And heard the tender crone
And what did I find at last
Light in that dark   fado
Within the tavern   a voice
Rustic   that sang like this

Beloved old guitar
Oh your ceaseless moaning
Eases my long torture
You're part of my own life
You lighten suffering
My soul feels your relief

When one day I set out
For good   eternity
The place I'm bound   recall
My sorrowful laments
I'll be beyond earshot
Yearning I'll feel no more
Be silent then guitar

JUDITH BARRINGTON

While trying to present the reader with poems that, I hope, carry a faint whiff of the Alfama, I was bitten by the Fado bug. This enchantment with the history, the music, the singers I have heard and watched, was the easy part; finding words in a new language and offering them to readers unfamiliar with the cultural context of Fado, was the challenge. The Alfama must always be in danger of seeming merely picturesque. The shallow tourist's view of the vibrant and deep art that is Fado seemed, as I struggled to unearth the true meanings of the songs, an ever-present pitfall; I remembered, for example, how crudely *flamenco* has been packaged in some of southern Spain's resorts – how it has been stripped of its *duende* to provide easy, upbeat entertainment. Yet, while I dreaded contributing to a disrespectful handling of the songs, I also had to admit that Fado *was* new to me, and that it would take years to understand the layers that lie beneath those stone alleys and haunting melodies. It was with this understanding that I finally could loosen my hold on the literal translations and try to write, in my own voice, poems inspired by, and borrowing from, the songs.

Lisboa Oxalá

Tal qual esta Lisboa, roupa posta à janela,
Tal qual esta Lisboa, roxa jacarandá,
Sei de uma outra Lisboa, de avental e chinela,
Ai Lisboa fadista de Alfama e oxalá.

Lisboa lisboeta da noite bem escura
De ruas feitas sombra, de noites e vielas,
Pisa o chão, pisa a pedra, pisa a vida que é dura,
Lisboa tão sozinha, de becos e ruelas.

Mas o rosto que espreita por detrás da cortina
É o rosto de outrora feito amor, feito agora.
Riso de maré viva numa boca ladina
Riso de maré cheia num beijo que demora.

E neste fado o deixo esquecido aqui ficar
Lisboa sem destino que o fado fez cantar,
Cidade marinheira sem ter de navegar
Caravela da noite que um dia vai chegar.

Lisbon, God Willing

Washing lines reach from window to window.
The air is fragrant with purple jacarandas.
And then there's a world within: Alfama with its Fado,
women in aprons and clogs, muttering *oxalá*.

All you who roam the city by night –
who slip along its shadowy narrow streets,
tread the stony ground of your hardscrabble life;
I know it's lonely there where the alleys lead nowhere.

But a face is watching from behind a curtain;
long ago, making love, it made this moment.
With persistent lips as time keeps on turning,
it laughs, greeting new waters with a lingering kiss.

I leave it hidden inside this song:
Lisbon whose fate no Fado can foretell.
City of sailors that never puts out to sea,
night ship that, *oxalá*, one day will reach the shore.

DAVID MOURÃO-FERREIRA

Maria Lisboa

É varina, usa chinela
Tem movimentos de gata;
Na canastra, a caravela,
No coração, a fragata...

Em vez de corvos no xaile
Gaivotas vêm pousar...
Quando o vento a leva ao baile
Baila no baile com o mar...

É de conchas o vestido,
Tem algas na cabeleira,
E nas velas o latido
Do motor de uma traineira...

Vende sonho e maresia,
Tempestades apregoa...
Seu nome próprio: Maria...
Seu apelido: Lisboa...

Maria Lisboa

She's a fishwife with wooden sandals
but her movements are feline.
Her basket sails along on her head,
her heart's a ship-o'-the-line...

> Her basket is a sailboat,
> her heart, a ship-o'-the-line.

On her shawl, instead of crows
seagulls come in to land ...
When the wind invites her to dance
she whirls and spins on the sand.

> When the wind invites her to dance,
> she spins and leaps on the sand.

Her dress is threaded with shells,
her hair tangled with seaweed,
she sails along with the throbbing
of a trawler's steady speed.

> Sailing along with the throbbing
> of a trawler's steady speed.

Hawking dreams and the smell of brine,
her cry is a storm's wild blast.
Maria is her first name
and Lisboa is her last.

> Maria is her first name
> Lisboa is the last.

DON PATERSON

Normally I take a very organic approach to the poetic version, but my tack with these poems was a little different, as I was acutely conscious of their relationship to song. Song – at least in English – has a very different sound-palette from poetry. So I tried to go for the middle way, hoping that the results would have some elements of both, and praying I wouldn't end up with something that was neither fish nor fowl. I deliberately made these versions quickly – again, the reverse of my usual approach; I've always liked the improvisatory feel and rough artefacts you get in song-lyrics, the way I like breath-noise and string-noise on recordings. In 'straight' poems, they'd have driven me crazy. 'A Luz de Lisboa' ('The Light of Lisbon') I tried to make more straightforwardly song-like, and went for a kind of six-line half-ballad; the conceit of the poem is fairly straightforward. 'A Minha Rua' ('My Road') was the most fun, and I ended up with a kind of Audenesque thing, which seemed right for its creepy litany; in my attempt to make it colloquial, some of the speech reflects the ungodly hybrid of Dundonian and Manhattanite spoken at home. 'O Espaço e o Tempo' ('Space and Time') is almost wholly incomprehensible and I couldn't for the life of me get it to make any sense, in the normal sense, but I hope that's the point; the tone of the original seems oracular and delirious. In the end I opted for a sort of Elizabethan conceit, and argued the thing out as if it were perfectly sensible – so the voice seems sane, even if what it's proposing is pretty crazy.

MANUELA DE FREITAS

A Luz de Lisboa (Claridade)

Quando Lisboa escurece
E devagar adormece
Acorda a luz que me guia
Olho a cidade e parece
Que é de tarde que amanhece
Que em Lisboa é sempre dia

Cidade sobrevivente
De um futuro sempre ausente
De um passado agreste e mudo
Quando mais te enches de gente
Mais te tornas transparente
Mais te redimes de tudo

Acordas-me adormecendo
E dos sonhos que vais tendo
Faço a minha realidade
E é de noite que eu acendo
A luz do dia que aprendo
Com a tua claridade

The Light of Lisbon

When Lisbon draws its shadows down
    the length of every lane
A new light rises through the town
    And wakes me up again
A second dawn dispels the night:
Lisbon never leaves the light.

City, you somehow survive
    a past that time deletes,
A future that will not arrive;
    The more folk fill your streets
The more invisible you seem:
there's nothing your light can't redeem.

Now your sleep's my waking day
    and from the dreams you turn
I make my bright reality.
    At dusk I start to burn
the new day that each day appears
in your eye, sleeping, open, clear.

MANUELA DE FREITAS

A Minha Rua

Mudou muito a minha rua
Quando o outono chegou
Deixou de se ver a lua
Todo o trânsito parou

Muitas portas estão fechadas
Já ninguém entra por elas
Não há roupas penduradas
Nem há cravos nas janelas

Não há marujos na esquina
De manhã não há mercado
Nunca mais vi a varina
A namorar com o soldado

O padeiro foi-se embora
Foi-se embora o professor
Na rua só passa agora
O abade e o doutor

O homem do realejo
Nunca mais por lá passou
O Tejo já não o vejo
Um grande prédio o tapou

O relógio da estação
Marca as horas em atraso
E o menino do pião
Anda a brincar ao acaso

A livraria fechou
A tasca tem outro dono
A minha rua mudou
Quando chegou o Outono

Há quem diga "ainda bem,
Está muito mais sossegada"
Não se vê quase ninguém
E não se ouve quase nada

Eu vou-lhes dando razão
Que lhes faça bom proveito
E só espero pelo verão
P'ra pôr a rua a meu jeito

My Road

What became of my road
when fall came this way?
The moon has been stowed
and the cars put away

All the houses are shrines,
they're so empty and still;
no clothes on the line
no flowers on the sill

No sign of life
down the market arcade
where I'd watch the fishwife
flirt with the trade

The cook's shot the crow,
and the teacher's gone west
You'll see no one now
but the nurse and the priest

The old organ-grinder
doesn't pass through
and the Tejo? Go find her —
grey clouds block the view

The station clock's stopped
and forgets every train
while that little kid's top
goes on spinning in vain

The bar has changed hands
and the bookstore's shut down
O my street's no man's land
since fall came to town

Good, some folk say
It's a much quieter place
It's true: look all day
and you won't see a face

So I just nod away
and pretend to agree
I know that come May
She'll be back. Come and see –

O Espaço e o Tempo

O tempo com que conto e não dispenso
Não limita o espaço do que sou
Por isso o aparente contrasenso
De tanto que te roubo e que te dou

No tempo que tenho te convenço
Que mesmo os teus limites ultrapasso
Sobras do tempo em que te pertenço
Mas cabes inteirinho no meu espaço

Não sei qual de nós dois veio atrasado
Ou qual dessas metades vou roubando
Entraste no meu tempo já fechado
Ganhando o espaço que me vai sobrando

Por isso não me firas com o teu grito
O espaço não dá tempo à solidão
Não queiras todo o tempo que eu habito
O espaço é infinito, o tempo não

Space and Time

The time that I require, my present tense,
can't circumscribe whatever makes me real,
the space of me – and so what makes no sense
is how much time I give, how much I steal.

So in the time I have, I'll show you how
even you can't hold me in my place.
But now I'm all yours, you're too much for now;
though somehow you contract to fit my space.

Times I don't know which half it is I steal,
or who came later – was it me or you?
You fell into my time already sealed,
and took the space I'd opened for the view.

So don't cut me with your cry, just let me be –
the one thing space can't give the time of day
is loneliness. Don't want a lifetime from me.
Space is infinite. Time speeds away.

GREY GOWRIE

In the 1970s I used to dine sometimes with the American poet Robert Lowell and his wife, the novelist Caroline Blackwood, at a Portuguese restaurant in Knightsbridge called O Fado. Lowell misspelt it, and couldn't be talked out of doing so, in his poem 'At Offado's'. A singer, a woman, would sing for ten or twelve minutes twice each evening. Although resistant to music in restaurants and nearly all 'folk music', I fell under the spell of Fado and remain there. To 'imitate' these three songs in English, I said each aloud, twice, in the Portuguese of one with a memory of Latin, and read literal translations four or five times. I then abandoned the text and riffed in English from memory through my love of the music. It is important to me that the titles remain in Portuguese. My English poems are riffs on Fado and the Latinate texture of the place-names within each lyric, as well as within the title of one of the poems, is important when I read them aloud – and they are written to be read aloud.

ANTÓNIO CALÉM

Lembras-te da Nossa Rua (Fado da Defesa)

Lembras-te da nossa rua,
Que hoje é minha e já foi tua,
Talhada para nós dois?
Foi aberta pela amizade,
Construída com saudade,
Para o amor morar depois.

Mas um dia tu partiste
E um vento frio e triste
Varreu toda a Primavera.
Agora veio o Outono
E as folhas ao abandono
Morreram à tua espera.

Certas noites o luar
Traça o caminho no mar
Para chegares até mim.
Mas é tão longa a viagem
Que só te vejo em miragem
Nas sombras do meu jardim.

E é nesta rua deserta
Que a minha alma então desperta
Só para ver-te passar.
Que importa ser a saudade
Que passeia na verdade
Aos olhos do meu sonhar?

Lembras-te da Nossa Rua (Fado da Defesa)

Remember our street?
Where we used to meet
and lived and loved in? Where you
used to live and I still do
and which was supposed to see us through?

A cold wind came,
cold even for springtime,
to sweep you away
like leaves that fell later
the autumn after

you'd gone. A sea
in moonlight brings you back to me
sometimes, but it is only
a mirage, a stratagem,
a ghost in my garden.

Our poor street
looks empty now it is too late
to find you. Sometimes
I imagine you coming and going
like you used to. But there is only the going.

ARTUR RIBEIRO

Vielas de Alfama

Horas mortas noite escura
Uma guitarra a trinar
Uma mulher a cantar
O seu fado de amargura.

E através da vidraça
Enegrecida e quebrada,
Aquela voz magoada
Q'entristece a quem lá passa

Vielas de Alfama
Ruas da Lisboa antiga...
Não há fado que não diga
Coisas do vosso passado

Vielas de Alfama
Beijadas pelo luar,
Quem me dera lá morar
P'ra viver junto do fado

A lua às vezes desperta
E apanha desprevenidas
Duas bocas muito unidas
Numa porta entreaberta

E então a lua, corada
Ciente da sua culpa,
Como quem pede desculpa
Esconde-se envergonhada

Vielas de Alfama
Beijadas pelo luar,
Quem me dera lá morar
P'ra viver junto do fado.

Vielas de Alfama

In dead hours of night
a guitar is trembling
and a woman singing
her bitter fado.

Even through the grimy
and murky glass
of her window
there comes a voice
for all who go
down alleys of Alfama,
streets of old Lisbon,
hurt by her sorrow.

I wish I lived there
too, for the fado.
I would spy, like the moon,
on secretive lovers
half-seen in doorways
or spurred on by sad
and shameful old songs

of the streets of Alfama,
alleys of Lisbon,
the moon, the guitar
and the woman singing.

FERNANDO PINTO DO AMARAL

Madrugada

Foi numa noite gelada,
Já rompia a madrugada
No momento em que eu te vi.
Não soube dizer-te nada
Nessa hora alucinada
E fiquei a olhar pra ti.

Andei p'las ruas à toa,
P'las vielas de Lisboa
Cada esquina sem ninguém.
Quando o amor nos abençoa
Há uma luz que perdoa,
Tanto mal que nos faz bem.

Nunca soube de quem era
Esse rosto que eu quisera
Guardar bem dentro de mim.
Talvez fosse uma quimera
Que ali me deixou à espera
Naquela noite sem fim.

Passou o tempo e agora
Volto a viver essa hora
Na cidade adormecida.
Mas quase rompendo a / ao romper da aurora
Há uma guitarra que chora
Saudades da minha vida.

Madrugada

Cold night with dawn breaking
like ice at the moment of waking
and your heart a dream window
you cannot look out of or know
whom to follow, where to go
and your love a shadow.

You drift on alone
through backstreets of Lisbon
empty as you are.
Is it worth walking so far
for some moral star,
for someone not there?

If only you knew
whom you wanted to make love to
in the end, or could come
to believe in the dream
she was the same
one you always suspected all the time.

The time that flows down
byways of a sleeping town
as each reiterating dawn
of your life wears on
to disappoint and inspire
your song, your sad guitar.

ELAINE FEINSTEIN

All translation of poetry is difficult, but these lyrics present a particularly daunting problem, since they are written to be *sung*. This means the question of syllables and patterns of stress is of great significance. Try to match the movement of the Portuguese line too exactly, and you will lose the natural word order on which English poetry depends. If you listen to Fado singers, however, the problem magically disappears. Great singers impose their own shape on any line they sing. So I have worked to find an *equivalent* to the melody of these particularly lovely lyrics; to give them a new music in English, which calls up the original, without seeking to imitate the verse, beat for beat.

There were other awkward decisions. Portuguese is a language very rich in guttural consonants, and easy rhymes – as in Spanish and Italian – which contemporary English poetry likes to avoid, if it disturbs the language of ordinary speech.

Altogether, my aim has been to make new English poems, while honouring the meaning of the lines, the simplicity of their cadences and their overwhelming demand to be sung.

JOSÉ CARLOS ARY DOS SANTOS

Rosa Da Noite

Vou pelas ruas da noite
com basalto de tristeza,
sem passeio que me acoite.
Rosa negra à portuguesa.

É por dentro do meu peito, triste,
que o silêncio se insinua, agreste.
Noite, noite que despiste
na ternura que me deste.

Um cão abandonado,
uma mulher sozinha.
Num caixote entornado
a mágoa que é só minha.

Levo aos ombros as esquinas,
trago varandas no peito,
e as pedras pequeninas
são a cama onde me deito.

És azul claro de dia,
e azul escuro de noite,
Lisboa sem alegria,
cada estrela é um açoite.

A queixa duma gata,
o grito duma porta.
No Tejo uma fragata
que me parece morta.

Morro aos bocados por ti,
cidade do meu tormento.
Nasci e cresci aqui,
sou amigo do teu vento.

Por isso digo: Lisboa, amiga,
cada rua é uma veia tensa,
por onde corre a cantiga
da minha voz que é imensa.

Rose of Night

As I walk the streets at night time
    my sadness is like basalt.
There's no pavement to protect me:
    Black rose of Portugal!

Silence makes a home inside me
    within my own unhappy chest.
Night, you have undressed yourself
    to give me tenderness.

I recognise my own pain now
    in some abandoned dog, or
any lonely woman –
    or an upturned rubbish bin.

On my shoulders I must carry
    your street corners and balconies.
The bed on which I lie down
    is made of cobblestones.

Light blue in the daylight,
    dark blue in the night time.
When Lisbon holds no happiness
    each star is like a blow.

Listen to a cat whine!
    Somewhere a door screams.
A frigate on the Tagus
    looks altogether dead,

I am dying piece by piece
    for you, tormenting city!
I was born here and grew up
    with your wind as my friend.

That's the reason I say: Lisbon,
    every street is a throbbing vein,
and along each one a song runs
    in my enormous voice.

JOSÉ CARLOS ARY DOS SANTOS

Alfama

Quando Lisboa anoitece
Como um veleiro sem velas
Alfama toda parece
Uma casa sem janelas
Aonde o povo arrefece.

É numa água-furtada
No espaço roubado à mágoa
Que Alfama fica fechada
Em quatro paredes de água
Quatro paredes de pranto
Quatro muros de ansiedade
Que à noite fazem o canto
Que se acende na cidade
Fechada em seu desencanto
Alfama cheira a saudade.

Alfama não cheira a fado
Cheira a povo, a solidão
A silêncio magoado
Sabe a tristeza com pão
Alfama não cheira a fado
Mas não tem outra canção

Alfama

When night falls over Lisbon
    then the whole of the Alfama
becomes a ship without sails, or
    a house without windows,
where people sit and grow cold.

And from some wretched garret
    stolen from Alfama's misery,
locked inside four walls of water
    – four stony walls of sobbing,
four walls of long disquiet –
    at night a song will soar out
which lights up the whole city!
    But Alfama, disenchanted,
still smells of melancholy.

It does not smell of fado
    but of solitary people
sitting in a wounded silence
    that tastes of bread and sadness.
Alfama does not smell of fado –
    but it has no other song.

JOSÉ CARLOS ARY DOS SANTOS

Fado dos Azulejos

Azulejos da cidade
Numa parede ou num banco
São ladrilhos da saudade
Vestida de azul e branco.

Bocados da minha vida
Todos vidrados de mágoa
Azulejos despedida
Dos meus olhos rasos de água.

À flor de um azulejo uma menina
Do outro um cão que ladra e um pastor
Ai! Moldura pequenina
Que és a banda desenhada
Nas paredes do amor.

Azulejos desbotados
Por quanto viram chorar
Azulejos tão cansados
Por quantos viram passar.

Podem dizer-vos que não
Podem querer-vos maltratar
De dentro do coração
Ninguém vos pode arrancar.

À flor dum azulejo um passarinho
Um cravo e um cavalo de brincar
Um coração com um espinho
Uma flor de azevinho
E uma cor azul luar

À flor dum azulejo a cor do Tejo
E um barco antigo ainda por largar
Distância que já não vejo
E enche Lisboa de infância
E enche Lisboa de mar.

The Tiles of Lisbon

Against a wall, or on a bench
    these tiles mark all our yearning
in blue and white ceramic:
    azulejos of Lisbon!

They are pieces of my own life,
    which has been glazed with sadness.
Let me say goodbye to each of them
    with tears in my eyes.

On one a little girl, the next
    a shepherd with his barking dog …
How every little frame becomes
    a single poignant moment
in the picture book of love …

Poor faded tiles, you've seen
    so many people crying!
How tired you must be
    of those who pass you by!

Some of them reject you, or even
    try to damage you
but I promise – you will never be
    torn out of my heart.

Look! on the surface of each tile:
    a carnation, or little bird,
a rocking horse, a pierced heart,
    a holly bush. Their colour
is always moonlight blue –

the colour of the river Tagus.
    There is an old boat on the shore –
I no longer see the distance –
    And it fills Lisbon with childhood,
it fills Lisbon with the sea!

PHILIP JENKINS

The principal concern in translating any poetry in which rhyme is important is to try to achieve the rhymes in English without producing something which is either forced or which sacrifices too much of the meaning of the original. My approach to these translations was to make a first poem in English which conveyed the meaning of the Portuguese original and then to let the rhymes emerge in the course of subsequent drafts.

Another concern is that in a Romance language like Portuguese the number of rhymes available for a single word will usually be greater than in English due to the conformity of noun and verb endings. Sure enough in these poems the poets use quite exacting rhyme schemes. While not always reproducing these exactly, I have consciously limited the number of rhymes in my English versions in order to reproduce the texture of the Portuguese originals.

The hardest single line I had to translate occurs in António Lobo Antunes's 'Valsa' ('Waltz'). The third line of the first verse in Portuguese is 'O mal que venha sempre o mar menor', literally 'Let evil always come as the lesser sea.' This is a very clever play on words requiring some explanation. The poet is punning on the Portuguese phrase 'o mal menor' – 'the lesser evil' – in the context of a series of metaphors associated with the sea that runs through the first two verses by speaking of 'o mar menor', the 'lesser sea'. This is an area of sea partly enclosed by land, like an inlet. It is as if the speaker in the poem is begging not to be separated from the beloved for a long time should the latter go to sea, preferring the 'lesser sea' as the 'lesser evil', since it implies a lesser degree of separation. But how was I to recreate this in my translation? In the end I chose something more explanatory at the expense of the wit of the original: 'May the sea not call you and we meet again.'

ANTÓNIO LOBO ANTUNES

Valsa

Ficámos finalmente meu amor
Na praia dos lençóis amarrotada
O mal que venha sempre o mar menor
Sorriso de vazante na almofada
O mal que venha sempre o mar menor
Sorriso de vazante na almofada

Se chamo som das ondas ao rumor
Dos passos dos vizinhos pela escada
É porque à noite acordo de terror
De me encontrar sem ti de madrugada
É porque à noite acordo de terror
De me encontrar sem ti de madrugada

Qual a cor desta noite e de que dedos
São feitas estas mãos que não me dás?
Oh meu amor a noite tem segredos
Que dizem coisas que não sou capaz
Oh meu amor a noite tem segredos
Que dizem coisas que não sou capaz

Waltz

My love we were left out of reach
On the sheets' dishevelled beach
May the sea not call you and we meet again
The smile of the ebb tide on the pillow
May the sea not call you and we meet again
The smile of the ebb tide on the pillow

If I describe the footsteps I hear outside
As the sound of waves reaching me here inside
It is because at night I wake up terrified
That you will be gone come the dawn
It is because at night I wake up terrified
That you will be gone come the dawn

What colour is this night and what fingers
Crown these hands whose refusal lingers?
Oh my love the night holds secrets
Which say things that I cannot say
Oh my love the night holds secrets
Which say things that I cannot say

JOSÉ RÉGIO

Fado Português

O fado nasceu um dia
Quando o vento mal bulia
E o céu o mar prolongava
Na amurada dum veleiro
No peito dum marinheiro
Que estando triste cantava
Que estando triste cantava

Ai, que lindeza tamanha
Meu chão, meu monte, meu vale,
De folhas, flores, frutas de oiro,
Vê se vês terras de Espanha
Areias de Portugal
Olhar ceguinho de choro

Na boca dum marinheiro
Do frágil barco veleiro
Morrendo a canção magoada
Diz o pungir dos desejos
Do lábio a queimar de beijos
Que beija o ar e mais nada
Que beija o ar e mais nada

Mãe, adeus, adeus, Maria
Guarda bem no teu sentido
Que aqui te faço uma jura
Que ou te levo à sacristia
Ou foi Deus que foi servido
Dar-me no mar sepultura

Ora eis que embora outro dia
Quando o vento nem bulia
E o céu o mar prolongava
À proa de outro veleiro
Velava outro marinheiro
Que estando triste cantava
Que estando triste cantava

Portuguese Fado

Fado was born one day
When the wind had all but died away
And the sky stretched out the sea
Along the gunwhale of a sailing boat
In a sailor's aching throat
As he turned his sadness into melody
As he turned his sadness into melody

Oh, what great beauty
There where my crop, my hill, my valley
Of leaves, flowers and golden fruits lie,
See if you can see the Spanish lands
Or even the Portuguese sands
Through the sweet tears that blind you in each eye

From the sailor's throat
In a fragile sailing boat
A painful song dying
Tells of the torment of desires
Of the lips aflame with kisses' fires
That kiss the air and then nothing
That kiss the air and then nothing

Mother, goodbye, Maria goodbye too,
Keep what I say now in mind
That here I make a pledge to you
That either I will marry you
Or in God's service I shall die
And be buried where the corals lie

And then even though on another day
When the wind had all but died away
And the sky drew out the sea
In the prow of another sailing boat
There sailed another sailor
Who turned his sadness into melody
Who turned his sadness into melody.

VASCO DE LIMA COUTO

Disse-te Adeus e Morri

Disse-te adeus e morri
E o cais vazio de ti
Aceitou novas marés
Gritos de búzios perdidos
Roubaram dos meus sentidos
A gaivota que tu és

Gaivota de asas paradas
Que não sente as madrugadas
E acorda a noite de chorar
Gaivota que não faz ninho
Porque perdeu o caminho
Onde aprendeu a sonhar

Preso no ventre do mar
O meu triste respirar
Sofre a invenção das horas
Pois na ausência que deixaste
Meu amor como ficaste
Meu amor como demoras.

I Said Goodbye to You and Died

I said goodbye to you and died
And the quay bereft of you
Accepted each new tide
Lost whelks' screams by the quayside
Stole from view
The seagull that is you

A seagull with wings that are still
That never sees dawn's gleam
And awakens the night with cries so shrill
A seagull that never nests and never will
Because it tore its memory's seam
In the place where it learned to dream

Imprisoned deep within the sea
Of sadness is my breathing made
The invention of time will not let me be
For in the absence you left for me
My love how you have stayed
Oh my love how you have stayed.

RUTH FAINLIGHT

The poetic resources of the Portuguese and English languages are very different, and the conventions governing poems and songs have little in common. In Fado, certain symbols and images – the 'gaivota' or seagull being an obvious example – have a meaning understood by every Portuguese listener, and religious ideas and imagery can still be invoked quite unselfconsciously. And on the technical level, the ease with which rhymes can be found in Portuguese is not the case in English. But this is not unique to the relationship between Portuguese and English – translating poetry from all the Romance languages presents the same problem.

After a first hearing of my three Fados, I listened to them several times more – mostly for the simple pleasure they gave me. Then I carefully read the texts, literals and notes, and studied the structure of the lyrics, their patterns and repetitions. I wanted to hear and understand the words clearly, to familiarise myself with the rhythm of the music and try to make my translation conform as far as possible to its melody. I even accompanied the singers (very much *sotto voce!*) with my own English versions to test whether or not they 'fit'. But as well as trying to make them work as songs, I know that they must read as poems on the page. As far as possible, I hope this has been achieved.

ALEXANDRE O'NEILL

Gaivota

Se uma gaivota viesse
Trazer-me o céu de Lisboa
No desenho que fizesse,
Nesse céu onde o olhar
É uma asa que não voa
Esmorece e cai no mar.

Que perfeito coração
No meu peito bateria
Meu amor na tua mão
Nessa mão onde cabia
Perfeito o meu coração.

Se um português marinheiro
Dos sete mares andarilho
Fosse quem sabe o primeiro
A contar-me o que inventasse
Se um olhar de novo brilho
No meu olhar se enlaçasse.

Que perfeito coração
No meu peito bateria
Meu amor na tua mão
Nessa mão onde cabia
Perfeito o meu coração.

Se ao dizer adeus à vida
As aves todas do céu
Me dessem na despedida
O teu olhar derradeiro
Esse olhar que era só teu
Amor que foste o primeiro

Que perfeito coração
Morreria no meu peito
Meu amor na tua mão
Nessa mão onde perfeito
Bateu o meu coração

Seagull

If a seagull came
And brought me the Lisbon sky
The drawing it would trace
Across that sky where your gaze
Is a wing which cannot fly
But falls mournfully to the sea

Such a perfect heart
Would beat in my breast
My love in your hand
That hand where my heart
Would be a perfect fit

If a Portuguese sailor
Voyager of the seven seas
Was maybe the first
To spin me his tall tales
If a new and brilliant gaze
With my gaze interlaced

Such a perfect heart
Would beat in my breast
My love in your hand
That hand where my heart
Would be a perfect fit

If all the birds in the sky
Bidding farewell to life
Brought me your final gaze
With their last goodbye
That gaze which was only yours
You my first love

Such a perfect heart
Would die in my breast
My love in your hand
That hand where my heart
Once perfectly beat

MANUELA DE FREITAS AND
JOSÉ MÁRIO BRANCO

Fado Penélope

Sagrado é este fado que te canto
Do fundo da minh'alma tecedeira
Da noite do meu tempo me levanto
E nasço feito dia à tua beira

Passei por tantas portas já fechadas
Co'a dor de me perder pelo caminho
A solidão germina nas mãos dadas
Que dão a liberdade ao passarinho

E enquanto o meu amor anda em viagem
Fazendo a guerra santa ao desespero
Eu encho o meu vazio de coragem
Fazendo e desfazendo o que não quero

A fome de estar vivo é tão intensa
Paixão que se alimenta do perigo
De o chão em que se inscreve a minha crença
Só ter por garantia ser antigo

Fado Penelope

I sing to you this sacred song
From the depth of my weaver's soul
From the night of my being I wake
Close by your side born into day

I pass so many doors already locked
Fearing I might lose my way
Solitude deepens as my hands unclasp
And grant the little bird its freedom

And while my love is voyaging
To wage a holy war on desperation
I fill my inner void with courage
Weaving then unweaving all I reject

The hunger for life is so intense
Passion nourished by uncertainty and danger
That the earth itself inscribed with my belief
Is the only guarantee of ancient tradition.

HENRIQUE RÊGO

Cabelo Branco é Saudade

Cabelo branco é saudade
Da mocidade perdida
Às vezes não é da idade
São os desgostos da vida

Amar demais é doidice
Amar de menos maldade
Rosto enrugado é velhice
Cabelo branco é saudade

Saudades são pombas brancas
A que nós damos guarida
Paraíso de lembranças
Da mocidade perdida

Se a neve cai ao de leve
Sem mesmo haver tempestade
O cabelo cor da neve
Às vezes não é da idade

Pior que o tempo em nos pôr
A cabeça embranquecida
São as loucuras d'amor
São os desgostos da vida

White Hair Means Yearning...

White hair means yearning
For youth's lost pleasures
Not only through age
But also life's sorrows

Too much love is madness
Too little love is hurtful
A wrinkled face means old age
White hair means yearning

Yearnings are white doves
Safely we'll guard them
Paradise of memories
Youth's lost pleasures

How gently the snow falls
No need for storm to rage
Hair the colour of snow
Not only through age

Worse than time's passage
Which whitens our heads
Are love's madness
And the sorrows of life

PASCALE PETIT

In each of Amália Rodrigues' lyrics I picked out the freshest images and played with them. While writing I often listened to the recited and sung lyrics I was provided with so my versions would be true to their spirit and their particular sorrowful tone. In 'Lágrima' ('Tear'), I was drawn to the simple but desolate image of a shawl cast on a floor. As the poem develops it is as if this shawl is the longed for single tear wrung from the unfeeling lover. What struck me most about 'Estranha Forma de Vida' was the idea of a heart independent of its owner's body and I wanted to amplify this. I visualised the heart as a surreal animal let loose from its ribcage and having to be recaptured. As this errant heart is the central image of my poem, I titled my version 'The Strange Heart'.

'Amor de Mel, Amor de Fel' ('Bitter Flower') was the hardest lyric to translate into a poem because it relies on that rhyme of *mel* and *fel*, and the English equivalents sweet and bitter love weren't fresh enough ideas for me to use. The sweet love is both honey and flower nectar. This gives way to sea and tear imagery. I depicted the subject of forbidden love as a double image of a rose and the sea. I imagined its petals as waves and its bitterness as saltwater. This bittersweet rose is also Fado sung in minor key – a synaesthetic third element. The love, being sinful, cannot be spoken, only sung. However, I could only sing it with words, not music, so I cut any repetitions of the lyrics which the music would have carried and instead expanded my triple image of the rose/sea/song.

AMÁLIA RODRIGUES

Lágrima

Cheia de penas
Cheia de penas me deito
E com mais penas me levanto,
No meu peito
Já me ficou no meu peito
Este jeito,
O jeito de te querer tanto,

Desespero,
Tenho p'ra meu desespero,
Dentro de mim,
Dentro de mim um castigo
Não te quero,
Eu digo que não te quero
E de noite,
De noite sonho contigo.

Se considero
Que um dia hei-de morrer,
No desespero
Que tenho de te não ver,
Estendo no chão,
Estendo no chão o meu xaile
E deixo-me adormecer

Se eu soubesse,
Se eu soubesse que morrendo
Tu me havias,
Tu me havias de chorar
Uma lágrima,
Por uma lágrima tua
Que alegria
Me deixaria matar

Tear

I go to bed tearless,
dry-eyed I wake.
I know that one day
I will die of not seeing you

so I spread my shawl,
my life's shawl
on the floor
and curl up inside.

If I thought
that my death
would draw
one tear from your eye,

just one drop –
I would cast myself down
on a murderer's floor
and beg to be killed.

I would open the shawl
of that drop
and drown in its fire.
For such bliss I would die.

AMÁLIA RODRIGUES

Estranha Forma de Vida

Foi por vontade de Deus
Que eu vivo nesta ansiedade.
Que todos os ais são meus,
Que é toda a minha saudade.
Foi por vontade de Deus.

Que estranha forma de vida
Tem este meu coração.
Vive de forma perdida.
Quem lhe daria o condão?
Que estranha forma de vida.

Coração independente,
Coração que não comando.
Vive perdido entre a gente,
Teimosamente sangrando,
Coração independente.

Eu não te acompanho mais,
Pára, deixa de bater.
Se não sabes aonde vais,
Porque teimas em correr,
Eu não te acompanho mais.

The Strange Heart

It's God's fault
I'm such a mess,
that I'm one big sigh,
one animal howl.
It's my creator's fault.

What a strange way my heart
has of escaping –
wilful and wild.
Who let it out?
What a strange beast it is.

Headstrong heart
you go your wounded way,
lost in the crowd,
stubbornly bleeding.
Headstrong heart

I won't be your keeper
so just stop beating!
Since you don't know where you're going
why keep running?
Come back to my ribcage.

AMÁLIA RODRIGUES

Amor de Mel, Amor de Fel

Tenho um amor
Oue não posso confessar
Mas posso chorar
Amor pecado, amor de amor
Amor de mel, amor de flor
Amor de fel, amor maior
Amor amado!

Tenho um amor
Amor de dor, amor maior
Amor chorado em tom menor
Em tom menor, maior o fado!
Choro a chorar
Tornando maior o mar
Não posso deixar de amar
O meu amor em pecado!

Foi andorinha
Que chegou no Primavera
Eu era quem era!
Amor pecado, amor de amor
Amor de mel, amor de flor
Amor de mel, amor maior
Amor amado!

Tenho um amor
Amor de dor, amor maior
Amor chorado em tom menor
Em tom menor, maior o fado!
Choro a chorar
Tornando maior o mar
Não posso deixar de amar
O meu amor em pecado!

Fado maior
Cantado em tom de menor
Em tom menor, maior o fado
Dor de um bem e mal amado!

Bitter Flower

There's a love
that can only be sung –
my fado rose
with thorns in major

hurts in minor.
My song has tears that swell the sea
but I can't stop mourning
my bitter briars.

Love was a swallow
that came in the spring
and I was who I was
when it blossomed sweet as brine

in an ocean of nectar.
My song loves pain –
pain's major key
but this must be cried quietly.

I cry a tide that swells the seas –
its major waves
break in minor
but I can't stop wanting

my springtide lover.
Fado in major sung in minor
opens the salt petals
of love's bitter flower.

FADY JOUDAH

A singer's voice creates new line breaks and emotional emphasis. This new linearity and repetition, as variation on refrain, guide my syntax toward new structure and relocation of emphasis: a translation as mimesis, impersonation, or an attempt at originality's illusion of shared simultaneity. In 'My Name Tastes to Me of Sand', 'mawaal' is an Arabic song form, performed a cappella, or with minor accompaniment, that shares the 'ghost of fado'. In 'Saudade Go Away', 'my heart is my only country' is a quote from Mahmoud Darwish's 'Eleven Planets at the End of the Andalusian Scene'.

VASCO DE LIMA COUTO

Meu Nome Sabe-me a Areia

Meu nome sabe-me a areia
Que cresce no rio novo
Entre as verdades que sonho
E as tristezas que transponho
Meu nome sabe-me a povo

Corro os caminhos do Mundo
Como o tronco de raiz
E se canto uma saudade
Eu limito a humanidade
Aos campos do meu país

Meu nome gastou os dias
Que eu tive de amor ao lado
Vivo a apagar uma estrela
E no desejo de vê-la
Meu nome sabe-me a fado

My Name Tastes to Me of Sand

My name tastes to me of sand, sand

piles at the bottom
of a newborn river
into truths I dream up and sorrows I overcome

I taste people on my tongue

my name grainy and like a forged trunk
it branches on the grid roads of the world

I sing a mawaal and yearn
I sing a mawaal and bind
humankind to the fields of my country

My name ran out of the days of love

My name ran out of the days when love
was by my side and now I live

to extinguish a star I desire to see
and in the desire my name tastes to me
of fado

JÚLIO DE SOUSA

Vim Para o Fado

VIM para o fado e fiquei
Sou corda duma guitarra
A que mais geme e soluça
Por alguém que usa samarra
E o mistério de uma capa
Que me tapa e me destapa
Se meu corpo se debruça

Se quizeres saber de mim
Quando não estou ao teu lado
Pergunta aos guardas da noite
Pergunta às mulheres compradas
Pergunta às portas fechadas
Pelo fantasma do fado.

E aos fadistas também,
Porque todos me conhecem
Mas se vires que me entristecem
Não digas á minha mãe

Já tenho novos amigos
Que me oferecem de beber
Mas ninguém mata esta sêde
Esta sêde de esquecer.

Vim para o fado e aqui,
Em cada noite perdida
Mais fado Há na minha vida
E mais me lembro de ti
Do amor que não te dei
Vim para o fado e fiquei.

I Came to Fado

I came to what was there
and stayed, became
a single string
of a guitar that moans and grieves
for one who wears a country fleece

A mysterious cape whichever way
I bend I am
exposed and concealed I am
when far

what night watchmen sketch
what paid-for women sense
what doors shut within rooms
a ghost of fado

Ask the fadistas and they'll tell you
I am, he is, as they
fling their sorrows into me

I fear for my mother tell her
or don't tell her

I have new friends that buy me drinks
and no one kills
this longing to forget
I came to fado and since I've come more fado
has gripped me each forlorn night

What I had and did not give

to you I've come to stay

JÚLIO DE SOUSA

Saudade Vai-te Embora

Olho a terra e olho o céu
E tudo me fala de ti
Do teu amor que perdi
Quando a minha alma se perdeu
Se a única verdade
Presente no nosso amor
Tem como imagem a cor
Tão bela e triste da saudade

Saudade vai-te embora
Ai de mim estou tão cansado
Leva para bem longe
Este meu fado
Ficou escrita no vento
Esta paixão
À noite o vento é meu irmão
Anda a esquecer a tempestade
Também quero olvidar
Esta saudade
Ai de mim que eu não consigo
Volta amor porque é verdade

Vai-se a dor fica a alegria
Vai-se o amor fica a amizade
Só não passa no meu peito
Esta profunda saudade
Porque será que não vens
Espreguiçar-te nos meus braços
Porque será que me tens
Na poeira dos teus passos.

Saudade Go Away

Earth and heaven deceive my gaze
               heaven and earth
I see only you
               what I lost when I lost my name
and the single truth
               a love an image
               the color of beautiful and sad
saudade   go away
go away saudade
               take this fate of yours
               this fate of mine
this passion
belongs to the wind
               the wind at night
says it's my brother, my kin

The wind remembers and forgets
the storm, and I
               too want to forget this saudade
               forgetfulness
is memory, enough
               reason for you
to return

The words say
               pain departs, joy lingers
               love ends, friendship loiters
saudade
               is my heart, my heart
               is my only country
and you still don't
               stretch your body
               awake between my arms

Am I the dust
               your footsteps leave behind

ALFRED CORN

Because Fado means 'fate', and the voices associated with the genre use high pitches, strong dynamics, and plangent melodic ornament, the common view is that its lyrics are all tragic or at least sad. Not so. Fado can deal with any sort of subject and often in the mode of irony or comedy. The three examples translated here are almost entirely comic in intention, and I've accentuated that aspect in my versions. Gabriel de Oliveira is among the best known artists in twentieth-century Fado, and his 'Senhora da Saúde' ('There's a Feast in Mouraria'), written in the 1930s, may well be his most famous lyric, admired for decades in a version sung by Amália Rodrigues. The Mouraria district in Lisbon, very ancient and traditionally working class, was and is the epicentre of Fado in the Portuguese capital. In the 1950s it was threatened with demolition when Lisbon city government tried to implement a plan of urban modernisation, but the effort was blocked, with Oliveira's song, among several others, mustered against the wrecking-ball. The Mouraria district came through intact, and to this day there is an annual procession in honour of Our Lady of Health – health being a practical concern in a quarter where sailors regularly sought out sex-workers. The nature of common experience in Mouraria is also discernible in the other lyrics by Oliveira translated here, 'Café de Camareiras' ('Café of Waitresses') and 'Foi na Travessa da Palha' ('Down in Haymarket Lane'), which need no glossing.

Fado, like popular song everywhere, is metrical and always rhymes. Metre in sung texts, though, is nearly always accentual rather than accentual-syllabic, and the numbers I've developed here are quite free, an approach that seems right for popular song. Rhyming them required ingenuity when proper names were involved; for example, 'Senhora da Saúde', which in one instance I translated as 'Our Lady of Health', and in another left in Portuguese. That was done as a rhyming convenience, certainly, but also in order to heighten the local flavour. I never doubted that rhyming was indispensable – so crucial, I felt, as to outrank in importance absolute fidelity to the literal meaning of the text. The working-class audience for Fado wouldn't see the point of an unrhymed lyric, indeed, such a departure might even be unconsciously regarded as an arrogant dismissal of the iron decrees of fate, for which metre and rhyme can serve as sonic emblems.

GABRIEL DE OLIVEIRA

Senhora da Saúde (Há Festa na Mouraria)

Há festa na Mouraria
É dia da procissão
Da Senhora da Saúde
Até a Rosa Maria
Da Rua do Capelão
Parece que tem virtude

Naquele bairro fadista
Calaram-se as guitarradas
Não se canta nesse dia
Velha tradição bairrista
Vibram no ar badaladas
Há festa na Mouraria

Colchas ricas nas janelas
Pétalas soltas no chão
Almas crentes povo rude
Anda a fé pelas vielas
É dia da procissão
Da Senhora da Saúde

Após um curto rumor
Profundo silêncio pesa
Por sobre o Largo da Guia
Passa a Virgem no andor
Tudo se ajoelha e reza
Até a Rosa Maria

Como que petrificada
Em fervorosa oração
É tal a sua atitude
Que a Rosa já desfolhada
Da Rua do Capelãos
Parece que tem virtude.

Our Lady of Health (A Feast in Mouraria)

A Feast in Mouraria:
It's the processional day
Of Our Lady of Health.
Even that Rose-Maria
Up from Chaplain Way
Has got holy by stealth.

In the hotbed of fado
Guitars nor people sing.
It's a strict decree, a
Custom from long ago.
But church bells ring and ring:
Feast Day in Mouraria.

At windows, rich tapestries;
Strewn petals in bright array;
And poor folks' gratitude.
Faith walks the ancient streets.
It's the processional day
Of Senhora da Saúde.

Loud noises for a space,
Then deep silence will fall
Over the Largo da Guia.
The Virgin on her dais
Floats past the kneeling faithful –
Including Rose-Maria.

It looks as though she froze,
Trying like hell to pray –
Her pose so calm, so pure,
Long-since-depetalled Rose
Up from Chaplain Way
Looks virginal once more.

GABRIEL DE OLIVEIRA

Café de Camareiras

Vou fazer a descrição
D'um café de camareiras
No Bairro da Mouraria
Lembrar tempos que lá vão
De fidalgos e rameiras
E cenas de valentia

Os rufias são actores
Do teatro da ralé
Por isso ninguém se ilude
Nós somos espectadores
E o teatro é o café
Do cantinho da saúde

E é bom que ninguém se afoite
Vão-se dar cenas canalhas
Nestes actos de má fé
Deram dez horas da noite
Entrou a rusga às navalhas
Pelas portas do café

Rufias falam calão
E uma camareira esperta
Chegou-se com ligeireza
P'ra mesa d'um rufião
Tirando a navalha aberta
Que ele espetara na mesa

Depois da rusga abalar
Entraram muitas rameiras
Há movimento Alegria
Há fadistas a cantar
Várias cenas desordeiras
Era assim a Mouraria

Café of Waitresses

I'm going to tell it like it was:
The Mouraria district was rough.
Girls waited table at cafés,
The brothers would hang out with whores
And prove (to some) that they were tough.
Let's hear it for the good old days!

Truth is, those 'gangstas' are actors,
Talking trash on a chavvy stage.
We listen but we don't believe.
Like, we are all just spectators
For little skits of hopped-up rage
In that dead-end street they call Relieve.

Good thing no major risks are run.
Yet, though these acts are mostly sham,
Some truly low-life scenes get played.
The café door bursts wide open
Just as the clock strikes ten pm:
Enter the weapon-search brigade.

One of the sharpest waitresses
(The brothers mumbling, 'What the fuck!')
Darts from her corner quick as a trout
To a table where this punter was.
The open switchblade that he's stuck
In the tabletop, she wrenches out.

At last the weapons goons depart.
Some twenty grinning tarts descend.
The joint's jumping in sheer delight.
Your fado crooners ply their art.
Chaotic scenes that never end –
The District on a typical night.

GABRIEL DE OLIVEIRA

Foi na Travessa da Palha

Foi na Travessa da Palha
Que o meu amante canalha
Fez sangrar meu coração
Trazendo ao lado outra amante
Vinha a gingar petulante
Em ar de provocação

Na taberna de friagem
Entre muita fadistagem
Enfrentei-os sem rancor
Porque a mulher que trazia
Concerteza não valia
Nem sombras do meu amor

P'ra ver quem tinha mais brio
Cantámos ao desafio
Eu e essa outra qualquer
Deixei-a a perder de vista
Mostrando ser mais fadista
Mais fadista e mais mulher

Foi uma cena vivida
De muitas da minha vida
Que não se esquecem depois
Só sei que de madrugada
Após a cena acabada
Voltámos para casa os dois

Down in Haymarket Lane

Down in Haymarket Lane
He filled my heart with pain,
That rascal, my boyfriend.
With a new girl at his side,
He flaunted his stupid pride,
Like he wanted to offend.

In that chilly tavern, loud
With the yelling fado crowd,
Calmly I gazed at them.
The slut that he now handled
No way could hold a candle
To the love I'd given him.

To prove who had more passion
We staged a competition,
Myself and that dumb one.
And I was ten times better!
At fado I outdid her,
But also as a woman.

Of the many I have seen,
That oft-remembered scene
Was like none I'd lived before.
And, meanwhile, let me say,
Before the break of day,
We were in love once more.

SARAH MAGUIRE

Songs and poems are very different animals (as anyone perusing a volume of lyrics-sans-music can attest) and, as a poet who's never aspired to song-writing and who's never rhymed anything other than my answering-machine message, I was uncertain whether I'd be capable of translating these delicate Fado songs with any degree of success.

I've co-translated a good deal of poetry (and one novel), largely from Arabic and Dari; and, in 2004, I founded The Poetry Translation Centre to translate contemporary poetry from Africa, Asia and Latin America to a high literary standard. The guiding principle of my own – and the Centre's – translations has always been to try to stay as close to the original poem as possible while attempting to produce something that functions as a new poem in English: to retain the 'foreignness' of the original poem while making it at home in its new language. And that's what I've tried to do with these Fado songs.

I did this by examining the Portuguese in detail. Although I can't speak Portuguese, I could make a little sense of it; and whenever I attempted or altered a line, I would look at the original, and the literal translations again. But, above all, I reminded myself that I was translating a *song*. And, arguably, what was the greatest help in the translation process, was listening to the recordings of the songs made from these lyrics. The mood of the songs – the jauntiness of 'Nasci Para Ser Ignorante' ('I Was Born to be Ignorant'), for example – was something I tried to reflect in my versions. I don't expect my translations to be sung to the music of the originals – as I said, I'm a poet, not a song-writer – but I do hope they have their own music, that they might sound 'singable'.

Nasci Para Ser Ignorante

Nasci para ser ignorante
mas os parentes teimaram
(e dali não arrancaram)
em fazer de mim estudante.

Que remédio? Obedeci.
Há já três lustros que estudo.
Aprender, aprendi tudo,
mas tudo desaprendi.

Perdi o nome às Estrelas,
aos nossos rios e aos de fora.
Confundo fauna com flora.
Atrapalham-me as parcelas.

Mas passo dias inteiros
a ver um rio passar.
Com aves e ondas do Mar
tenho amores verdadeiros.

Rebrilha sempre uma Estrela
por sobre o meu parapeito;
pois não sou eu que me deito
sem ter falado com ela.

Conheço mais de mil flores.
Elas conhecem-me a mim.
Só não sei como em latim
as crismaram os doutores.

No entanto sou promovido,
mal haja lugar aberto,
a mestre: julgam-me esperto,
inteligente e sabido.

O pior é se um director
espreita p'la fechadura:
lá se vai licenciatura
se ouve as lições do doutor.

Lá se vai o ordenado
de truta-e-meia por mês.
Lá fico eu de uma vez
um Poeta desempregado.

Se me não lograr o fado
porém, com tais directores,
e de rios, aves e flores
somente for vigiado,

enquanto as aulas correrem
não sentirei calafrios,
que flores, aves e rios
ignorante é que me querem.

I Was Born to Be Ignorant

I was born to be ignorant
Yet my parents insisted
(They really put their foot down)
On making me a student.

I could do nothing but obey
And for three years now I've studied.
To learn, I have learned everything –
And everything's been unlearned.

I forgot the names of stars
And rivers – every one –
I mix flora up with fauna,
And I stumble over numbers.

And yet for days on end
I'll watch a river drifting past.
My true loves will remain
The birds and the waves.

A star always shines
Through my window pane
Because I won't go to bed
Without wishing it good night.

I'm well known to the flowers
And can name them in their thousands,
Yet I still have no idea
What doctors christened them in Latin.

Even so I'll be promoted
The minute there's an opening:
They're all convinced I'm smart,
Intelligent and wise.

What I dread most is the boss
Listening at the keyhole:
For there goes my certificate
If he hears *this* doctor's lessons,

There go my wages
Of peanuts per month.
And then, once again,
I'll be a poet with no job.

If that doesn't happen
And the directors forget me,
I will only be spied on
By birds, rivers and flowers.

I will not feel frightened
While my lessons continue
Because birds, rivers and flowers
Know I'm born to be ignorant.

AGUSTINA BESSA-LUÍS

Garras dos Sentidos

Não quero cantar amores,
Amores são passos perdidos,
São frios raios solares,
Verdes garras dos sentidos.

São cavalos corredores
Com asas de ferro e chumbo,
Caídos nas águas fundas,
Não quero cantar amores.

Paraísos proibidos,
Contentamentos injustos,
Feliz adversidade,
Amores são passos perdidos.

São demências dos olhares,
Alegre festa de pranto,
São furor obediente,
São frios raios solares.

Da má sorte defendidos
Os homens de bom juízo
Têm nas mãos prodigiosas
Verdes garras dos sentidos.

Não quero cantar amores
Nem falar dos seus motivos.

Love Claws at the Senses

I don't want to sing of love
Love is a path that's lost
Love is the sun gone cold
Love claws at the senses

A stampeding horse
With wings of iron and lead
Plunged into deep water –
I don't want to sing of love

Forbidden paradise
Unjust contentment
Happy adversity –
Love is a path that's lost

Demented vision
Festival of misery
Compliant commotion
Love is the sun gone cold

Defended against misfortune
Those men of sound judgement
Have in their prodigious grasp
Love that claws at the senses

I don't want to sing of love
Nor consider its motives

ANTÓNIO BOTTO

Canção

Pelos que andaram no amor
Amarrados ao desejo
De conquistar a verdade
Nos movimentos de um beijo;
Pelos que arderam na chama
Da ilusão de vencer
E ficaram nas ruínas
Do seu falhado heroísmo
Tentando ainda viver!,
Pela ambição que perturba
E arrasta os homens à Guerra
De resultados fatais!,
Pelas lágrimas serenas
Dos que não sabem sorrir
E resignados, suicidam
Seus humaníssimos ais!
Pelo mistério subtil,
Imponderável, divino,
De um silêncio, de uma flor!,
Pela beleza que eu amo
E o meu olhar adivinha,
Por tudo o que a vida encerra
E a morte sabe guardar
– Bendito seja o destino
Que Deus tem para nos dar!

Song

For those who've turned to love
Firm in the belief
Of conquering the truth
In the impulse of a kiss

For those who have been burned
By the illusion of success
Yet live on in the ruins
Of their disastrous dreams
Determined to survive

For the ambitions that unsettle
And incite men to war
With fatal results

For the quiet tears of those
Who've forgotten how to smile
Who resign their pain to suicide

For the mysteries,
Imponderable, divine,
Of silence, of a flower

For the beauty I adore
And gaze at, in wonder

For everything in life
That death knows how to guard

– I bless the destiny
That God has given us!

ERIC ORMSBY

I found these three Fado poems to be completely captivating. I was intrigued particularly by the apparent simplicity of the language joined to the complexity of the emotions expressed. The themes were conventional but highly nuanced; there was tenderness and bitterness, anger and affection, sarcasm and sadness, as well as sly humour – sometimes, it seemed, all at once. I came to realize that when Guilherme Pereira da Rosa wrote the lines in 'A Viela' (to quote from the literal trot), 'It was Fado, but Fado/Is not always what people think!' he was not exaggerating in the least. This impression became even stronger when I listened to the poems as they were read and then again, when I heard them sung; both the readers and the singers somehow managed to convey tones which ordinarily would appear at odds with one another; it reminded me a bit of hearing a violinist play double-stops, except that sometimes the 'stops' sounded triple or even quadruple. Of course, it's a commonplace to say that Fado is as joyous as it's melancholy; but I was surprised to discover that, however sad the songs, the chief impression I took from listening to them was one of a certain grave jubilation. Still, the more I read them, the more I listened to them, the more I despaired of being able to capture even the smallest sense of this complexity in my translations. At first I thought about using the original poems as 'occasions' for rather free versions, simply writing new poems on the themes and motifs of the Portuguese originals (and I might still do this for my own purposes). But then I was so struck by the beauty of the Fado songs – their distinctive music as poems, quite apart from the actual music – that I decided that I had to attempt versions that were as faithful as I could make them to the originals. I kept all the rhyme schemes and I tried to catch something of the rhythms (though I often had to alter this in certain ways), but what I like to think of as the 'emotional polyphony' of the songs proved hardest to recreate in English. I couldn't always avoid emphasising one emotion, one tone, one nuance, over another which seemed to be equally present. I was probably too often tempted to use an English verb or a noun which seemed flashy in comparison with the original. I suspect that that temptation arose in part because of the great difference between English and Portuguese; it's hard to write so simply in English without falling into banality. I was struck too by the wonderful play in Portuguese between the quick, often slanting quality of the vowels, especially the nasal vowels, and the rich sloshiness of the consonants, all those sh's and z's! In several lines or stanzas I tried to reproduce this effect in English – discreetly, I hope! – if only to give some feeling for the lovely and intricate texture of the Portuguese.

GUILHERME PEREIRA DA ROSA

A Viela

Fui de viela em viela
Numa delas dei com ela
E quedei-me, enfeitiçado.
Sob a luz d'um candeeiro,
Estava ali o Fado inteiro,
Pois toda ela era Fado!

Arvorei um ar gingão,
Um certo ar fadistão,
Que qualquer homem assume,
Pois confesso que aguardei,
Quando por ela passei,
O convite do costume!

Em vez disso, no entanto,
No seu rosto só vi pranto,
Só vi desgosto e descrença!
Fui-me embora amargurado:
Era Fado, mas o Fado
Não é sempre o que se pensa!

Ainda recordo agora
A visão que ao ir-me embora
Guardei da mulher perdida.
Na pena que me desgarra,
Mais me lembra uma guitarra
A chorar penas da vida!

In the Alleyway

As I wandered past each alleyway
I saw her in the fading day.
She stood beyond the shadow,
Alone in the gas-lamp's light,
And I stopped, spellbound by the sight:
Ah, Fado, I thought, *she's all Fado!*

I swayed in full bravado,
I struck that stance of Fado
Every red-blooded man understands.
I expected solicitation,
The back-alley invitation
Where sweaty cruzados change hands.

Instead, to my surprise,
I saw hot tears in her eyes,
I saw grief, I saw shattered illusions,
And I turned away in distress.
She was Fado, bittersweet Fado, yes,
Which refuses our cozy conclusions.

I still can call to mind
The vision of that blind
Sorrow and the terrible tears
In her eyes, and still they sting
Like a guitar whose grieving string
Cries down all the lost lanes of the years.

MARIA DO ROSÁRIO PEDREIRA

Pontas Soltas

Dizem que já não me queres,
Que há outro na tua vida
E que é dele que tu gostas.
São as línguas das mulheres
Que vinham lamber-me a ferida
Se me virasses as costas.

Se eu não levo isso a peito
Nem olho para a desdita
Como coisa que se veja,
Tu tens de perder o jeito
De ser sempre a mais bonita
E despertar tanta inveja.

Dizem que já me enganaste,
Soprando no meu ouvido
Fados de rara beleza.
Não sei se me atraiçoaste,
Mas eu senti-me traído
Mesmo sem ter a certeza.

Nada disto acontecia
Se desses as tuas voltas
Sempre, sempre, ao meu redor.
Tens de perder a mania
De deixar as pontas soltas
Na história do nosso amor.

Loose Ends

The women with their silky tongues
Gossip as they lick my wounds.
They say you don't fancy me anymore.
They croon it in their songs.
They even say you've found
Somebody new as your paramour.

If I snap my fingers and sigh,
If I say it's no disaster,
If I'm a pillar of nonchalance,
That's only because I know you'll try
To dim those flashes of your lustre
That summon envy out of every glance.

Ah, they lisp seductive fados
In bold whispers in my ear.
They say you've been unfaithful more than once.
They say it's time we sang our sweet adieux.
To hell with them: I love you still though still I fear
You've fitted me with more horns than a dunce.

Sweetheart, it's time you made amends.
It's high time you stopped flitting here and there.
I mean to be the midpoint of your pirouettes.
It's time you stitched together those loose ends,
It's time you made a promise to repair
Our poor love's broken bits.

AUGUSTO DE SOUSA

Amor é Água que Corre

Amor é água que corre
Tudo passa, tudo morre
Que me importa a mim morrer
Adeus cabecita louca
Hei-de esquecer tua boca
Na boca d'outra mulher

Amor é sonho, é encanto
Queixa mágoa, riso ou pranto
Que duns lindos olhos jorre
Mas tem curta duração
Nas fontes da ilusão
Amor é água que corre

Amor é triste lamento
Que levado p'lo vento
Ao longe se vai perder
E assim se foi tua jura
Se já não tenho ventura
Que me importa a mim morrer

Foi efémero o desejo
Do teu coração que vejo
No bulicio se treslouca
Onde nascer a indiferença
Há-de morrer minha crença
Adeus cabecita louca

Tudo é vário neste mundo
Mesmo o amor mais profundo
De dia a dia se apouca
Segue a estrada degradante
Que na boca d'outra amante
Hei-de esquecer tua boca

Hei-de esquecer teu amor
O teu corpo encantador
Que minha alma já não quer
Hei-de apagar a paixão
Que me queima o coração
Na boca d'outra mulher

Love is Water...

Love is water: it races away,
It dies as it races, it will not stay.
Will I still give a damn when it dies?
I'll forget all your kisses
In a new lover's caresses.
My little madcap, no teary goodbyes!

Love is dream, love is charm;
It twists the heart to laughter then alarm.
The tears that roll from your pretty eyes
Form fountains where illusion
Drops in sparkles of confusion.
Love is water and it races till it dies.

Love's a melancholy song
But it doesn't last for long.
It's lifted by the wind and sent
In all directions till it's lost.
Like all your promises, it's tempest-tossed.
But ah, as to dying, I'm indifferent.

For you, so brief of wing,
Desire was a butterfly thing.
Tipsy in tumult it bred
Disdain and indifference
Till loving no longer made sense.
Farewell, my little silly-head!

This world is all a tangle,
True love is left to dangle;
It dwindles day after day.
Down the bad path it descends
To where all loving ends
And it fades in another's embraces away.

Now I'll learn forgetfulness,
Now I'll learn to efface your caress,
I'll teach my heart oblivion
And stamp on every ember
It burns me to remember.
I will lose you at last in some other woman.

FIONA SAMPSON

That all translation involves translation-of-context is a cliché, of course. Still, it got to be that way because it's clearly true. At the most practical level, when a translator asks herself, 'What am I doing?' she needs some working theory of *what kind of thing* she might be moving from or to. This Fado project has allowed us to hear 'our' songs in context. It's even glossed their iconography... in short, if translation is a form of armchair travel, this has been a luxury cruise. But still: all poetry, including vernacular verse, centrally has to do with – makes itself available for – private, personal meaning. And the translator brings that kind of meaning to bear, too. For me, Fado means speeding across the snow-covered plain of Pannonia towards the ruined bridges and factories of Novi Sad. It's January 2001. Milosevic has been gone for three months. My companion, a Portugophile Serb who handles his UNHCR four-wheel drive as if death were either so likely or so inconceivable as to be beside the point, plays Madredeus continually, and the music's reach and plangency seems to ventriloquise that landscape, muted under its enormous sky – and the whole tragic country. I know Fado is urban, maritime and Mediterranean: but to me it will also always be full of an insatiable, collective grief. Grief doesn't concern itself with looking pretty. I've tried, therefore, to let the archetypal stories in these three songs speak as clearly and simply as possible.

HENRIQUE RÊGO

O Lenço

O lenço que me ofertaste
Tinha um coração no meio
Quando ao nosso amor faltaste
Eu fui-me ao lenço e rasguei-o.

Ainda me lembro esse lenço
Vindo do teu seio túmido
Escondi-o ainda húmido
No peito de fogo intenso.

Esse acaso, hoje penso
No qual infantil receio,
Muito orgulhoso, guardei-o
Lamento a minha loucura
Porque esse lenço o perjura
Tinha um coração no meio.

Esse coração bordado
Por triste sina era o meu
E por isso ele morreu
Quando o lenço foi rasgado
Foi-se a chama do passado
Pois em cinzas sepultaste
Este amor que atraiçoaste
O que serve a dor incalma
Vesti de luto a minha alma
Quando ao nosso amor faltaste.

Beijos, sorrisos e afagos
Me deste hei-de esquecê-los
Pois os seus doces desvelos
Com meus beijos foram pagos
Teus olhos eram dois lagos
Lascivo era o teu seio
Foi tudo efémero enleio
Breve e fugaz ilusão
Magoaste-me o coração
Eu fui-me ao lenço e rasguei-o.

The Scarf

The scarf you gave me
had a heart at its heart
When you cheated our love
I took that scarf and tore it up

I remember how this scarf
came from your swelling breast
still damp – I hid it
in my burning chest

Today, thinking
how I guarded it proudly
with childish anxiety,
I lament my obsession –
because this scarf perjured itself
with the heart at its heart

Sad fate –
that embroidered heart was mine
and so it died
when the scarf was torn up
That old flame died down
as you heaped ashes
on the love you betrayed –
What use protesting pain?
I dressed my soul in black
when you cheated our love

You gave me kisses, smiles and strokes –
I'll forget them
because those sweet attentions
were bought with my kisses
Your eyes were two pools,
your breast sensuous –
everything a momentary folly
a brief and fleeting illusion
You broke my heart
I took that scarf and tore it up

AMADEU DO VALE

Fado do Ciúme

Se não esqueceste
O amor que me dedicaste
O que escreveste
Nas cartas que me mandaste
Esquece o passado
E volta para meu lado
Porque já estás perdoado
De tudo o que me chamaste

Volta meu querido
Volta como disseste
Arrependido
De tudo o que me fizeste
Haja o que houver
Já basta p'ra meu castigo
Essa mulher
Que andava agora contigo

Se é contrafeito
Não voltes toma cautela
Porque eu aceito
Que vivas antes com ela
Pois podes crer
Que antes prefiro morrer
Do que contigo viver
Sabendo que gostas dela

Só o que eu peço
É uma recordação
Se é que mereço
Um pouco de compaixão
Deixa ficar
O teu retrato comigo
P'ra eu pensar
Que ainda vivo contigo

Fado of Jealousy

If you've not forgotten
the love you swore me,
what you wrote
in the letters you sent me,
forget the past
and turn back to me
For you're forgiven everything
because you chose me

Turn back my darling
Turn back like you said,
regretting
all you've done to me
Whatever's happened
that woman
going around with you
is punishment enough

If that's not who you are
and you don't turn back –
take care! I might agree
you belong with her instead
For you'd better believe
that I prefer to die
than live with you
knowing you desire her

All I ask
is one memento –
if I deserve
a little compassion –
Leave your picture
with me
so I can think
that I still live with you

ALDINA DUARTE

A Voz do Silêncio

No silêncio outra voz
Ao lado duma canção
Repartida entre nós
Tem a força de uma oração

Cada qual deve encontrar
Seu caminho desejado
Há um céu para alcançar
Sem virtude e sem pecado

Anda a dor devagarinho
Num coração apressado
Quando o amor fala baixinho
Tristemente amordaçado

Gota a gota na varanda
Seca a chuva distraída
Quem nos pede quem nos manda
Não dar voz à própria vida

The Voice of Silence

In the silence another voice
A song close by
Shared between us
it has the force of a prayer

Every one must find
their own way
There's a heaven to be won
beyond virtue and sin

Pain stalks
the racing heart
when gagged and grief-struck
love whispers –

Drop by drop the oblivious rain
dries on the terrace
Who demands, who commands us
not to give voice to life?

GEORGE SZIRTES

I think Fado has some similarities in mood to the French chanson and the 1930s and 40s Hungarian popular song. That's how it seemed to me and that thought helped. I was, of course, keen that the translations should be singable and noticed that there was room for some mild enjambment in the originals. The way the Fado melody springs forward or hangs back seems to allow for that. The greatest problem, as it often is with songs dealing with direct emotion and strong declarations, was to avoid sounding trite or grandiose in English. It is, I think, generally the case that so-called simple song, the popularly poetic, moves the heart deeply in the original language because that heart already possesses the depth and wealth of association with which to equip it. The heart recognises itself in it. Writing good apparently simple songs takes genius. Translating the three I had, I found two of them – 'Toada do Desengano' ('Melody of Disenchantment') and 'Fado de Tristeza' ('Fado of Sadness') – had to be allowed emotional room in some places and held back a little in others. I could not help thinking partly of Elizabethan song and partly of Auden's words for songs. They were my chief English style-guide. There was also, I felt, a rationale, an argument proceeding through all three and if I could keep the argument going the discipline would prevent the English words becoming vapid. Some lines are a gift. Such was 'composed of yes, composed of but' (in my version of 'Toada do Desengano') which has a tough logical ring to it. If I trusted that, I felt, the song would have backbone. The longest and most complex of the three songs was 'Trova do Vento que Passa' ('Ballad of the Wind Passing By'). Here it was the precision of the imagery as well as the mounting argument that would hold things together: the balance between nostalgia, anger and hope. The political context was pretty clear albeit in symbolic form.

The urban nature of Fado is particularly attractive to my urban imagination, and though I have never been to Lisbon, seeing the city in the film *Mariza and the Story of Fado*, it felt very close to my heart. The technical elements of rhythm and rhyme were no more challenging here than in many other poems. It was the tone, always the tone, that mattered most – the tone as it appeared in English.

As a footnote, there is a tendency among Hungarians to wish that they were Portuguese. 'If we had a more fortunate history we might have been Portugal' they think. One of the younger contemporary playwrights had considerable success with a play he called simply *Portugal* in which provincial Hungarians idealise Portugal.

VASCO GRAÇA MOURA

toada do desengano

este amor, este meu fado,
tão vivido e magoado
entre o sim e o todavia,
este amor desgovernado,
marcado a fogo e calcado
em funda melancolia

este amor dilacerado,
este amor que noite e dia
me arrebata e me agonia,
este amor desenganado,
de saudades macerado,
a encher-me a vida vazia,

este amor alucinado,
este amor que desvaria
entre o luto e a alegria,
sendo assim desencontrado
meu amor desesperado,
que outro amor eu cantaria?

Melody of Disenchantment

My fado and my love I sing
Borne out of life and suffering
Composed of yes, composed of but,
Unruly love, unbound and rash.
Once burning flame, now heap of ash
Trodden deep into the rut.

Love torn and shredded, torn and gone
Love that has ever swept me on
Both day and night and hurts like hell
Love undeceived that knows the cost
Love tortured by what's known and lost
That fills life like an empty well.

This bedlam love, these fevered dreams
Of love that madden with their screams
Of happiness and suffering
This love that won't be made to fit
That's desperate beyond its wit
What other love is there to sing?

MANUELA DE FREITAS

Fado da Tristeza

Não cantes alegrias a fingir
Se alguma dor existir
A roer dentro da toca
    Deixa a tristeza saír
    Pois só se aprende a sorrir
    Com a verdade na boca

Quem canta uma alegria que não tem
Não conta nada a ninguém
Fala verdade a mentir
    Cada alegria que inventas
    Mata a verdade que tentas
    Porque é tentar a fingir

Não cantes alegrias de encomenda
Que a vida não se remenda
Com morte que não morreu
    Canta da cabeça aos pés
    Canta co'aquilo que és
    Só podes dar o que é teu

Fado of Sadness

No false joy now, sing what is due
To pain, since pain oppresses you
Make the sharp teeth of loss your song
    So give it vent, so let it go
    True smiles are learned by those who know
    The taste of truth upon the tongue.

To sing of joys you don't possess
Says nothing though in fancy dress
The very truth is made of lies
    That murder truth with each false claim
    To joys that don't deserve the name
    So with pretence the true joy dies.

Don't sing to order, joys won't serve
False comforters who don't deserve
A cure for death that isn't real.
    Let your whole body sing the truth
    Of which your being is the proof
    Give what you are, sing what you feel.

MANUEL ALEGRE

Trova do Vento que Passa

Pergunto ao vento que passa
notícias do meu país
e o vento cala a desgraça
o vento nada me diz.

Pergunto aos rios que levam
tanto sonho à flor das águas
e os rios não me sossegam
levam sonhos deixam mágoas.

Levam sonhos deixam mágoas
ai rios do meu país
minha pátria à flor das águas
para onde vais? Ninguém diz.

Se o verde trevo desfolhas
pede notícias e diz
ao trevo de quatro folhas
que morro por meu país.

Pergunto à gente que passa
por que vai de olhos no chão.
Silêncio – é tudo o que tem
quem vive na servidão.

Vi florir os verdes ramos
direitos e ao céu voltados.
E a quem gosta de ter amos
vi sempre os ombros curvados.

E o vento não me diz nada
ninguém diz nada de novo.
Vi minha pátria pregada
nos braços em cruz do povo.

Vi minha pátria na margem
dos rios que vão pró mar
como quem ama a viagem
mas tem sempre de ficar.

Vi navios a partir
(minha pátria à flor das águas)
vi minha pátria florir
(verdes folhas verdes mágoas).

Há quem te queira ignorada
e fale pátria em teu nome.
Eu vi-te crucificada
nos braços negros da fome.

E o vento não me diz nada
só o silêncio persiste.
Vi minha pátria parada
à beira de um rio triste.

Ninguém diz nada de novo
se notícias vou pedindo
nas mãos vazias do povo
vi minha pátria florindo.

Também nascem flores no esterco
(Diz quem ganha em te perder)
Eu é por ti que me perco
Perder-me assim é viver

E a noite cresce por dentro
dos homens do meu país.
Peço notícias ao vento
e o vento nada me diz.

Quatro folhas tem o trevo
Liberdade quatro sílabas
Não sabem ler é verdade
aqueles para quem eu escrevo.

Mas há sempre uma candeia
dentro da própria desgraça
Há sempre alguém que semeia
canções no vento que passa

Mesmo na noite mais triste
em tempo de servidão
há sempre alguém que resiste
há sempre alguém que diz não.

Ballad of the Wind Passing By

I ask the passing wind for news
Of how my people fare
But wind keeps silence on the truth
And speaks of no despair.

I ask the rivers on which dreams
Are carried down the flood
But there's no calm in that rough stream
Just sorrow and bad blood.

They carry dreams but leave behind
Nothing of home but tears.
Oh rivers, what comfort will you find?
When no one ever hears.

Take a green clover, tear off leaves
And bring me some reply.
And tell the four-leaved clover it is
For my country that I die.

Men cast their eyes down as they go,
I question their sullen mood.
Silence: the only answer they know
To life in servitude.

I saw a green branch in splendour thrust
its head high, spread and glow.
Those who obey a tyrant must
Walk with their heads bent low.

The wind keeps silent as the grave,
There's no news from my land.
A crucified country where people have
Nails driven through the hand.

I saw my fatherland on the banks
Of rivers flowing past
Like one who loves to travel but
Is doomed to stay stuck fast.

I saw ships setting out in power
(my fatherland set fair)
I saw my country in full flower
(green leaves and green despair)

Some there are who would ignore
Your name or call it cursed.
I saw you on the dark cross you bore
In the arms of hunger and thirst.

And still the wind says nothing
The silence seems forever.
My fatherland stands moping
By the side of the sad river.

To ask for news is little use
For speech there's little room.
But I've seen empty hands produce
A fatherland in bloom.

Flowers may grow in dung, say those
For whom your loss is gain.
It is for you that I must lose
My life to live again.

Night in my country enters hearts
And takes up residence there.
I ask the wind with all its arts
For news but there's only air.

The clover has four leaves and four
Syllables has the word.
Li-ber-da-de. What can't be read
Can at least be heard.

My readers can't read but there is light
In the bleakest fate we bear.
Someone will always sow the bright
Song in the passing air.

In the saddest night there still remains,
Despite the tyrant's blow,
Someone who stands straight in his chains,
Someone who answers No.

MARILYN HACKER

My three poems are 'imitations' rather than translations, using the three lyrics I was given as a jumping-off place for the imagination (something I rarely if ever permit myself when working as a translator of poetry in the strict sense).

These three Fado poems are imbued with *saudade*, that untranslatable word implying longing, desire and loss of something which, in some uncertain future, might be regained, a poetics of displacement that I could not avoid associating with (for example) some of Mahmoud Darwish's lyrics set to music and sung by Marcel Khalifé or the Joubran Brothers. That's my explanation for having transplanted two of these poems to another landscape, and made of David Mourão-Ferreira's young woman on her rooftop balcony in Alfama someone whose name is also a 'dawn' in another language.

Beitounia is a large town with about 20,000 inhabitants, about four kilometers southwest of Ramallah, whose main livelihood was the cultivation of the adjacent olive groves, grapevines and wheatfields. 17,000 dunnams (over four thousand acres) of its agricultural lands were effectively confiscated by the erection of the Israeli Separation (or Apartheid) Wall in 2004. On 30 March 2004, a group of 150 citizens of Beitounia, joined by twenty international and Israeli peace activists, held a nonviolent demonstration called 'Palestinian Land Day', which ended in an unprovoked attack by Israeli soldiers ... and the wall construction continued.

David Mourão-Ferreira's Fado poem 'Libertação' ('Tahrîr') is not, of course, a ghazal, as I transformed it in my 'imitation', but it shares with the ghazal a disjunction among its short quatrain stanzas, encircling and implying rather than narrating fragments of a story, further informed by the title.

Amália Rodrigues, when she sang many or most of these lyrics, was not a young woman, nor am I, and I allowed that particular *saudade* to inform my version of 'Barco Negro' ('Black Boat').

DAVID MOURÃO-FERREIRA

Madrugada de Alfama

Mora num beco de Alfama
E chamam-lhe a madrugada
Mas ela de tão estouvada
Nem sabe como se chama

Mora numa água-furtada
Que é a mais alta de Alfama
E que o sol primeiro inflama
Quando acorda a madrugada
Mora numa água-furtada
Que é a mais alta de Alfama

Nem mesmo na Madragoa
Ninguém compete com ela
Que do alto da janela
Tão cedo beija Lisboa

E a sua colcha amarela
Faz inveja à Madragoa
Madragoa não perdoa
Que madruguem mais do que ela
E a sua colcha amarela
Faz inveja à Madragoa

Mora num beco de Alfama
E chamam-lhe a madrugada
São mastros de luz doirada
Os ferros de sua cama

E a sua colcha amarela
A brilhar sobre Lisboa
É como a estátua de proa
Que anuncia a caravela
A sua colcha amarela
A brilhar sobre Lisboa

Sahar al-Beitounia

After David Mourão-Ferreira's 'Madrugada de Alfama'

She lives in Beitounia
And her name is Sahar
Her name is the hour
Between sunrise and morning.

Her bougainvillea
Overlooks Beitounia
Where a mango-bright bedspread
Hangs over the railing
Lit by first light
That reflects from a wall.

Not the wall of a house
Or her family's orchard.
She can see the graffiti
Ich bin ein Berliner.

Marwân had orchards
Al-zaytûn wa-l-'inab
Olive trees, grapevines,
Where they went out to work
Between sunrise and morning.

She is *bint Marwân*
(and also *bint Su'âd*).
She is *ukht Târiq,*
Ukht Mahmûd, ukht Asmâ.

When jeeps and bulldozers
Converged on Beitounia
A hundred and twenty
All walked out at midday
Were chased back with teargas
And rubberized bullets.

Seventeen thousand dunnams
Of orchards and wheatfields
With a wall thrust between them
And the doors of Beitounia.

Her name is Sahar
At dawn in Beitounia
Where the first light reflects
On the wall of a prison.

Ismuhâ Sahar
Bayn al-fajr wa-l-subh
– her name is Sahar,
between sunrise and morning.

DAVID MOURÃO-FERREIRA

Libertação

Fui à praia, e vi nos limos
a nossa vida enredada.
Ó meu amor, se fugirmos,
ninguém saberá de nada!

Na esquina de cada rua,
uma sombra nos espreita.
E nos olhares se insinua,
de repente, uma suspeita.

Fui ao campo, e vi os ramos
decepados e torcidos!
Ó meu amor, se ficamos,
pobres dos nossos sentidos!

Hão-de transformar o Mar
deste amor numa lagoa:
e de lodo hão-de a cercar,
porque o mundo não perdoa.

Em tudo vejo fronteiras,
fronteiras ao nosso amor!
Longe daqui, onde queiras,!
a vida será maior!

Nem as espiranças do céu
me conseguem demover.
Este amor é teu e meu:
só na terra o queremos ter.

Tahrîr

After David Mourão-Ferreira's 'Libertação'

Through the skein of years, I had nothing to fear from this place.
How final and brief it would be to disappear from this place.

The tangle of driftwood and Coke cans and kelp in the sand
made me think of the muddle that drove us (my dear) from this
place.

An orchard, a vineyard, a stable, a river. A wall.
The impassable distance today once seemed simple and near
from this place.

There was the word *refuge,* there was the word *refugee*
who, confused and disrupted, began to appear from this place.

The silence that lasted for decades, for months or for hours
will sooner or later be broken. You'll hear from this place.

There is a wall, and the words that we write on the wall.
Libertação! Can you make out *Tahrîr* from this place?

From your bedroom window with the sun coming up
I could see dusty jitneys crawl towards the frontier from this place.

My name's rhyme with yours and the things that are done in our
names
in whatever writing no longer sounds terribly clear from this place.

DAVID MOURÃO-FERREIRA

Barco Negro

De manhã que medo
que me achasses feia
acordei tremendo
deitada na areia.

Mas logo os teus olhos disseram que não
E o sol penetrou no meu coração.

Vi depois numa rocha, uma cruz
e o teu barco negro dançava na luz
vi teu braço acenando entre as velas já soltas
dizem as velhas da praia que não voltas,
são loucas, são loucas.

Eu sei meu amor
que nem chegaste a partir
pois tudo em meu redor
me diz que estás sempre comigo.

No vento que lança
areia nos vidros
na água que canta
no fogo mortiço
no calor do leito
nos bancos vazios
dentro do meu peito
estás sempre comigo.

Black Boat

After David Mourão-Ferreira's 'Barco Negro'

If you were there when I woke
With my barbed wire, with my scars,
You would avert your green gaze
I would feel the chill of regret

Though you said something else
In sunlight, over wine.

I saw a cross on a tall rock
And a black boat danced on light
Someone waved, was it you,
A brown arm between white sails.

Old women know
That more go away
Than will ever return
Than the morning has scars.

In the wind as it blows
Wet sand against the panes
On the water that sings
In the fire as it dies
In blue sheets warmed by
Someone sleeping alone
On an empty park bench
When they lock up the square
You are still there

Brown arm green gaze black boat blown sand barbed wire.

CAROL RUMENS

This project was a fascinating challenge, because it required a translation double-act – to turn a poetic song in one language into a song-like poem in another. In modern English, poems are rarely song-like. Yet I felt that, in order to be true to the spirit of Fado, my poems should aspire towards melody. I thought about the ballad as the natural English form of poetic song, and that simple rhythmic structure underlies all my translations, particularly, perhaps, the quatrains of 'Fria Claridade' ('Cold Brightness').

The latter is a beautiful song, expressing intense, almost raw, personal emotion. The melody and lyrics are seamlessly welded. The narrative and its imagery are almost archetypal. My early versions tended to be too literary, and when I aimed for greater simplicity, I ran the risk of seeming banal. Nevertheless, I felt it would be better to err on the side of vernacular simplicity. I began with full ABAB rhymes and a regular metrical beat, but then loosened both rhyme and rhythm. As I redrafted the poem I gradually moved back closer to the original. Finally, I even kept the inversion of 'Grande, grande era a cidade', because it enhances the emotion so poignantly.

What I particularly liked about 'Fria Claridade' was that the speaker is not always central. Grammatically, and perhaps mimetically, the 'I' is often a small, uncertain figure. The light is larger than the speaker: the stranger's eyes have their own existence, independent, it seems, of the speaker's perception. I tried to capture this in the second verse, where the eyes are personified as 'passers-by'.

The other songs seemed more malleable. In 'Havemos de Ir a Viana' ('We Shall Go to Viana'), the challenge was to convey the tension underlying the romance and jauntiness. The subtext is political exile. The censor is looking over the poet's shoulder. This is why I changed 'sombras misteriosas', 'mysterious shadows' to 'deceitful shadows'. I hoped to suggest a darker atmosphere than the words themselves conjure in English.

'Povo que Lavas no Rio' ('You that Wash Clothes in the River') is an impassioned, declarative poem that contains a wealth of concrete detail. Whereas in 'Fria Claridade' the four-line stanza had been hard to fill in English, here, the six-line stanza with its denser narrative and descriptive content, seemed the right-sized vessel for its new language.

Padding is always the first monster lying in wait for the translator. The second is a clash of registers – that awful, grinding jolt when you allow different styles of diction to jostle together. I hope I evaded these beasts, but at the moment I am too close to the work to be sure.

I tried to use assonance and alliteration in all the poems. The English language can never sing *bel canto* like a Romance language, but rhythmic emphasis allied to the repetition of sounds can help its recalcitrant music to emerge.

PEDRO HOMEM DE MELLO

Fria Claridade

No meio da claridade
Daquele tão triste dia
Grande grande era a cidade
E ninguém me conhecia

Então passaram por mim
Dois olhos lindos depois
Julguei sonhar vendo enfim
Dois olhos como há só dois

Em todos os meus sentidos
Tive preságios de Deus
E aqueles olhos tão lindos
Afastaram-se dos meus

Acordei a claridade
Fez-se maior e mais fria
Grande grande era a cidade
E ninguém me conhecia

Cold Brightness

In the light of that saddest day,
Vast, vast was the city.
No one returned my gaze.
Not one person knew me.

Then, in a dream come true,
Two beautiful passers-by
Appeared in front of me – two
Unique, unrepeatable eyes!

My senses trembled. God
Himself seemed to make a promise.
But the eyes had no sooner held
My own, than they vanished.

I woke on the saddest day,
And icy light pierced through me.
Vast, vast was the city.
Not one person knew me.

PEDRO HOMEM DE MELLO

Havemos de Ir a Viana

Entre sombras misteriosas
Em rompendo ao longe estrelas
Trocaremos nossas rosas
Para depois esquecê-las

Se o meu sangue não me engana
Como engana a fantasia
Havemos de ir a Viana
Ó meu amor de algum dia
Ó meu amor de algum dia
Havemos de ir a Viana
Se o meu sangue não me engana
Havemos de ir a Viana

Partamos de flor ao peito
Que o amor é como o vento
Quem pára perde-lhe o jeito
E morre a todo o momento

Se o meu sangue não me engana
Como engana a fantasia
Havemos de ir a Viana
Ó meu amor de algum dia
Ó meu amor de algum dia
Havemos de ir a Viana
Se o meu sangue não me engana
Havemos de ir a Viana

Ciganos verdes ciganos
Deixai-me com esta crença
Os pecados têm vinte anos
Os remorsos têm oitenta

We Shall go to Viana

Among deceitful shadows
When far-off stars are breaking,
We'll give each other roses –
To forget we ever gave them.

I feel it in my bones –
If I'm not self-deceiving,
We're going to Viana.
Oh, my some-day darling,
My darling love-to-be,
We're going to Viana.
If I'm not make-believing,
We'll be leaving for Viana.

We'll wear a button-hole
And we'll leave without a sigh
For the wind must not stand still,
And love that waits will die.

I feel it in my bones,
And if I'm not just dreaming
We'll be going to Viana.
Oh, my some-day darling,
My darling love-to-be,
We're going to Viana.
If I'm not make-believing,
We shall go to Viana!

Gypsies, green young gypsies,
Let this motto be my fate:
Sins are boys of twenty:
Regrets are ten times eight!

PEDRO HOMEM DE MELLO

Povo que Lavas no Rio

Povo que lavas no rio
Que talhas com teu machado
As tábuas do meu caixão
Pode haver quem te defenda
Quem compre o teu chão sagrado
Mas a tua vida não.

Fui ter à mesa redonda
Beber em malga que esconda
Um beijo de mão em mão
Era o vinho que me deste
Água pura fruto agreste
Mas a tua vida não.

Aromas de urze e de lama
Dormi com eles na cama
Tive a mesma condição
Povo povo eu te pertenço
Deste-me alturas de incenso
Mas a tua vida não.

Povo que lavas no rio
Que talhas com teu machado
As tábuas do meu caixão
Pode haver quem te defenda
Quem compre o teu chão sagrado
Mas a tua vida não.

You that Wash Clothes in the River …

You that wash clothes in the river,
You that chop planks with machetes,
Cutting my coffin to size –
There may be some who save you;
They buy up the land God gave you,
But your life, nobody buys.

At the round table we mingled,
And drank from the bowl that circled
With covert kisses and wine.
You gave me clean water, wild berries.
You shared your feast, but your life,
Your life, nobody buys.

I sleep in the simplest bed,
Steeped in aromas of mud
And heather, the same as my people.
I lie where the poorest lies,
And you bless me with sweet-smelling incense,
But your life, nobody buys.

You that wash clothes in the river,
You that chop planks with machetes,
Cutting my coffin to size –
There may be some who save you;
They buy up the land God gave you,
But your life, nobody buys.

DAVID CONSTANTINE

I like the idea of *desgarrada*, a session in which *fadistas* improvise against each other. Seems to me a very good image of what goes on when one poet translates another. The song calls forth its answer, across the languages. And really all poetic translation, even if you keep close, is an answering back, in your own tongue. It's a self-assertion against an original which, however much you love and admire it, you must in some way contradict. To make a poem in your own language you have to assert your freedom from the foreign poem to which your poem is in the first place beholden for its very life.

Learning about *desgarrada* encouraged me to do what I should have had to do anyway in translating these three songs. I had to make something of them out of my own life. This was particularly clear to me when I addressed 'Lisboa Antiga' ('Old Town'). I'm ashamed to say that I've never been to Lisbon (though after this exercise and having heard the Fado songs I'd like to) and to come near the feeling in the song I 'translated' Lisbon into my home town, Salford. There in my own and my mother's memories I was on familiar ground. Forgive me, Lisbon! In translating 'Mãos Sujas' ('Dirty Hands') I kept closer, but 'answered back' by making these workers justly angry. I shifted the song into revolt. The images in 'O Sonho' ('The Dream') were congenial to me. I arranged and concentrated them into a narrative I could call my own. I remembered the bull-leapers of Minoan Crete from thirty years ago and the *razeteurs* of Arles from a month ago. As to Severa, I guess most poets and lovers of poetry know a good deal about her, in one or other of her many incarnations.

In truth, I don't speak Portuguese so I have done these singers less than justice. But I feel them to be generous. They will go on singing and surely won't mind if now and then a foreigner answers back.

JOSÉ GALHARDO AND AMADEU DO VALE

Lisboa Antiga

Lisboa velha cidade
Cheia de encanto e beleza
Sempre a sorrir tão formosa
E ao vestir sempre airosa
O branco véu da saudade
Cobre o teu rosto linda princesa

Olhai, senhores,
Esta Lisboa doutras eras
Dos cinco réis das esperas
E das toiradas reais
Das festas das seculares procissões
Dos populares pregões
Matinais
Que já não voltam mais.

Lisboa d'oiro e de prata
Outra mais linda não vejo
Eternamente
A brincar
E a cantar
De contente
Teu semblante se retrata
No azul cristalino do Tejo

Olhai, senhores,
Esta Lisboa doutras eras
Dos cinco réis das esperas
E das toiradas reais
Das festas das seculares procissões
Dos populares pregões
Matinais
Que já não voltam mais.

Old Town

Old town, dirty old town
Thirty-five miles from the sea
But from there to us
Through the buttercup fields and the moss
The big ships crept
And stepped up the great canal
Trailing gulls, and believe you me
That was a sight to see!

Dirty old town
Smog in the mornings, the buses came
Like timid beasts being led
By Master, the bus conductor,
Walking slowly ahead.
And when we came home
Wide-eyed from the glittering Christmas pantomime
Oh the lamps had haloes of rain.

The big ships passed
Big as tenements through
The placid cows in the fields
And there was a lock
We could bike it to
Where the jovial idle singing sailors threw
Us oranges down
That were meant for market in the dirty old town.

And courting couples rode home
On the top of the Number 9 bus
From a Sunday walking out
In the bluebell woods.
Oh armfuls of bluebells came down
Like streams from the slopes of the hills
Into the dirty old town.

FREDERICO DE BRITO

Mãos Sujas

Mãos sujas do suor, mãos negras do trabalho,
Penhor da gente humilde, o seu melhor brazão,
São quem maneja a serra e quem empunha o malho,
São quem desbrava a terra e quem semeia o pão!.

Queimaram-nas de sol, as seifas dos trigais,
Tingiram-nas de mosto as dornas dos lagares
Andaram na montanha a derrubar pinhais,
Nas galeras de sonho, atravessaram mares!.

Ter as mãos sujas de trabalho, é ser alguém;
O que só pode acontecer aos homens sãos!.
Tenho as mãos sujas? – Que me importa?. Ainda bem!.
E ai de quem não tem coragem de sujar um dia as mãos!.

Mãos sujas do suor e do carvão das minas
Mas que sabem rezar ao toque das Trindades;
Mãos que na rocha negra e áspera das colinas
Ergueram catedrais, aldeias e cidades!.

Mãos que um dia na França, olhando a Pátria Mãe,
Pegaram num clarim, tocando a unir fileiras;
Andaram arranhando a "Terra de ninguém"
E amassaram com sangue o barro das trincheiras!.

Dirty Hands

Our hands are dirtied by the dirty work we do.
We raise our hands for sale. We ask what will you bid
For hands that know the saw, the hammer, sickle, plough
And break the land and sow the seed that gives you bread.

Our hands that grasp the sickle, the strong sun burns them brown.
Turning the grapes to wine, see how it stains our hands.
We climb the mountain slopes, we cut the tall trees down
For ships to bring you wealth from other people's lands.

You praise our hands and say the work of them is good.
You take and take from us. When did you ever give?
Dirt cheap you get our work, dirt cheap our sweat and blood.
Little you know, little you care what lives we live.

There's coal under the skin of the hands that dig your mines
And sweat falls on the hands we clasp at the angelus.
We build you palaces on hills above the plains
So we look up to you and you look down on us.

And for the land you own and call our Motherland
You taught our hands to shoot, gas, stab our brothers dead
And bleeding there with them in a land called No Man's Land
We clenched and squeezed the clay as though we kneaded bread.

Our dirty hands are strong. The work of them is good.
The day will come when they will take and you will give.
We'll have fair wages then for our work and sweat and blood
And you will pay us dear for the lives you made us live.

FRANCISCO DUARTE FERREIRA
(RADAMANTO)

O Sonho

Na minha cama, só, estava deitada,
Mas sem poder dormir, pus-me a sonhar...
Eu sonho muitas vezes acordada...
E o que sonhei, então, vou-vos contar:

Era uma tarde linda... Vinham toiros
Correndo estrada fora, para a praça,
Onde os toureiros vão procurar loiros,
Entusiamando ao rubro a populaça!...

Eu andava para ali, entontecida
Pelo sol, pela cor, pela algazarra,
De repente, porém, fui atraída
Pelo doce trinar de uma guitarra;

Era o fado... Mas, Fado rigoroso,
Cantava-o a Severa com preceito
E a guitarra, nas mãos do Vimioso,
Punha anseios de fogo no meu peito!...

Senti-me então fadista como era
A rascôa cigana, e quiz cantar:
– Cantei ao desafio co'a Severa!...
–... Mas, isto, meus senhores, foi a sonhar!...

The Dream

All day day-dreaming, you would think there'd be
By nightfall not an ounce of dream left in my head
But hear this, friends, last night, the dream that came to me
Alone as always in my sad white double bed.

Hot afternoon, the bulls, crowds roaring, and alone
I am the one who dares. They watch me stroll and halt
And beckon him, the stamper, and when his head goes down
A horn in either hand, I vault, I somersault,

And take the favour in my teeth! Next thing I know,
Soft dusk in that sweet town, I'm strolling where I please,
Wearing the bull's cockade and suddenly Vamioso
Beckons me down a lane of pomegranate trees

And there she is, Severa, the Fado girl! Let's see,
She says, smiling, bull-running boy, are you the man
When I lift my white throat to sing loud back at me
While the lord here plays? I am, oh friends, I can,

The gypsy tongue is mine, louder the old lord plays
And we go throat to throat, she and I, five hours and more
My songs for hers and hers for mine. Dreamer, she says,
Listen for me tomorrow singing at your bedroom door.

ACKNOWLEDGEMENTS

The Calouste Gulbenkian Foundation would like to thank all the poets or the estates of the poets who have given permission for their work to be included in and translated for the anthology and also the Portuguese Society of Authors for permission to publish and translate the work of the poets they represent. While every effort has been made to secure permission to reprint material protected by copyright, the Foundation will be pleased to make good any omissions brought to its attention in future printings of this book.

The publication of *Saudade* has been a huge collaborative endeavour and would have been impossible without the support, expertise and advice of many individuals and organisations. The Foundation is especially grateful to Helena Almeida, Laurinda Alves, Alzira Arouca, Joaquim Pais de Brito (Museu Nacional de Etnologia), Liliana Costa, Pedro Cruz (Sociedade Portuguesa de Autores), O Fado restaurant, Shreela Ghosh (Free Word Centre), Alda Goes (Fonoteca Municpal de Lisboa), Grey Gowrie, Gill Hedley, Ana Cristina Louro, Francisco Mendes, Vasco Graça Moura, Helder Moutinho, Rui Vieira Nery, Filipa Oliveira, Sara Pereira (Museu do Fado), Ian Ritchie (City of London Festival), Teresa Salomé and Telmo Tenente (D. Quixote).

PORTUGUESE POETS

Manuel Alegre (b. 1936) is a Portuguese politician and poet who graduated in Law from Coimbra University and became part of the Coimbra Fado scene. Sent to fight in Angola during the Portuguese colonial war, he protested against the conflict, was arrested by the secret police and lived in exile in Algiers until the 1974 revolution. He then joined the Socialist Party, rose to Vice President of the Portuguese Parliament and was a candidate for the presidency of the republic in 2007. As a poet, Alegre has achieved much popular and critical acclaim.

Fernando Pinto do Amaral (b. 1960) is Professor of Romance Literatures at the University of Lisbon and a poet, novelist and award-winning translator. Recently, he has been challenged by the Fado singer Carlos do Carmo to write for the genre, helping to create a bridge between tradition and modernity, and in 2008 received the Goya Award for Best Original Song for 'Fado da Saudade' sung by Carlos do Carmo in the film *Fado*. His first novel was *The Secret of Leonardo Volpi* (Don Quixote, 2009).

António Lobo Antunes (b. 1942) is an internationally renowned Portuguese novelist, often tipped for the Nobel Prize. Although from childhood he had wanted to be a writer, Antunes was sent to medical school and became a doctor, later specialising in psychiatry. During the Portuguese colonial war, he served in an army hospital in Angola, an experience which had a profound effect on his writing. He has won numerous prizes for his work and continues to be a practicing psychiatrist as well as pursuing his writing, which, unknown to many, includes poetry.

João Linhares Barbosa (1893–1965) was a prolific Fado poet, author of more than 3,000 poems. He started publishing his work in the paper *A Voz do Operário* (*The Labourer's Voice*) and in 1922 founded *Guitarra de Portugal,* the first and most influential of a series of publications entirely dedicated to Fado. This made hundreds of poems available to anyone interested, considerably expanding the Fado repertoire.

Agustina Bessa-Luís (b. 1922) is one of the most important figures in Portuguese contemporary literature. A prolific novelist with over fifty books published, she has received numerous national and international awards and occupied top positions in a number of arts organisations. Some of her books have been adapted to the screen by leading Portuguese filmmaker Manoel de Oliveira, a close friend.

António Botto (1892–1959) was an eccentric writer who grew up in the Alfama district of Lisbon, which deeply influenced his work. Although poorly educated, he worked for a time as a bookshop clerk, acquainting himself with many of Lisbon's men of letters. He became a civil servant and worked in Angola, but was expelled for misconduct on his return to Lisbon. His fourth book of poems *Canções* gained attention when Fernando Pessoa wrote an article praising the author's courage for openly singing about homosexual love. There was a scandal and Botto attained lifelong notoriety. He survived by writing articles, and doing radio shows and poetry readings, first in Portugal and later in Brazil.

José Mário Branco (b. 1942) is a singer-songwriter who became well known as part of the 'intervention song' movement that was popular in Portugal after the 1974 revolution ended 48 years of fascist dictatorship. Branco is also an accomplished producer and has been working with the Fado star Camané for a number of years.

Frederico de Brito (1894–1977) was a cab driver, composer and poet who created over 1,000 poems and hundreds of tunes during his career. At the age of eight he began writing Fado lyrics for his older brother. Later in his career, Amália Rodrigues, Alfredo Marceneiro, Carlos do Carmo (who popularised Branco's great classic 'Canoas do Tejo') and other leading Fado singers ensured the reputation of his work.

António Calem (1913–91) was born into an old family of Port wine producers in Oporto and published several books of poetry in the 1940s and 50s. His best-known poem for Fado was the 'Fado da Defesa', set to music by the Earl of Sabrosa and a hallmark of the repertory of Maria Teresa de Noronha.

Vasco de Lima Couto (1924–80) was an established poet whose repertoire included Fado lyrics made popular by singers such as Amália Rodrigues, Carlos do Carmo and Max. Originally from Oporto, he also lived in Angola and Mozambique before returning to settle in Lisbon. As well as writing, he loved reading poetry and acting, which he did professionally, performing at Lisbon's Teatro Nacional D. Maria II.

Aldina Duarte (b. 1967) is a Fado singer of the same generation as Mariza and Camané, to whom Duarte was married. She also worked as a researcher at EMI Music Portugal, organising the company's immense archives of Portuguese music, much of which comprises Fado recordings. Duarte's poems are interpreted by herself and a number of her contemporary *fadistas*, including Camané, Pedro Moutinho, Mariza and António Zambujo.

Francisco Duarte Ferreira (Radamanto) (1908–72) was one of the most representative of a genuinely 'popular' tradition of Fado poetry (with Linhares Barbosa and Henrique Rego, for example), during the golden era of Fado music in the 1920s and 30s. This tradition was in contrast to the work of the erudite poets who came to Fado through the influence of Amália.

Manuela de Freitas (b. 1940) is a successful film actress and a poet whose lyrics are often sung by the Fado star Camané.

José Galhardo (1915–67) was a lawyer, poet, playwright of approximately 150 plays, and director of the Portuguese Society of Authors. A number of his Fado poems became very popular, in particular his French version of the classic 'Coimbra, Avril au Portugal'.

Sebastião da Gama (1924–52) was a Professor of Portuguese and poet whose work focused on nature, especially the Sierra Mountains where he lived. He founded the League for the Protection of Nature in 1948 and died young from tuberculosis, which had afflicted him since childhood. In 1999 a new National Poetry Prize was inaugurated in his name.

Nuno Júdice (b. 1949) is an award-winning poet, writer and essayist and currently Professor at the New University of Lisbon. Since 1997 he has also been a cultural adviser to the Portuguese embassy in Paris and director of the Instituto Camões. Like Fernando Pinto do Amaral, Júdice has been challenged by the Fado singer Carlos do Carmo to write for the genre, helping to create a bridge between tradition and Fado in the twenty-first century.

Pedro Homem de Mello (1904–84) was an aristocrat who studied law in Coimbra and Lisbon and later became a prolific poet. Fed monarchic, conservative and catholic ideals since childhood, he was particularly fond of and close to the people (mainly the peasants), who were often the subject matter of his poems. This interest led him to become a specialist in Portuguese traditional music. He was one of the prestigious poets whose work Amália Rodrigues chose to sing, a decision that played an important role in the redefinition of Fado in the 1960s.

Vasco Graça Moura (b. 1942) is a lawyer, writer, translator and politician who is currently a Member of the European Parliament, representing the Portuguese Social Democratic Party. He is an expert in Fado poetry and has also written poems for the younger generation of *fadistas*.

David Mourão-Ferreira (1927–96) was a Lisbon-born university professor and writer who became one of Portugal's greatest twentieth-century poets. In 1963 he was elected secretary-general of the Portuguese Society of Authors and later became president of the Portuguese Association of Writers. In the 1960s, Mourão-Ferreira and contemporaries like Pedro Homem de Mello and Alexandre O'Neill were the first to produce erudite poetry for Fado, transforming the genre. In 1996 he received the Prix Career Consecration of the Portuguese Society of Authors.

Artur Ribeiro (1924–82) was a Fado poet, singer and composer, writing over 300 songs and 700 poems during his lifetime. In the 1940s he became a celebrated singer with the Estoril Casino Orchestra in Lisbon, and began to compose regularly with the pianist Mario Teixeira. In 1948 Ribeiro met Max, for whom he wrote some of his greatest hits, including 'Ilha da Madeira'. He was a regular on the APA radio programmes and also wrote music for films. Many leading *fadistas* of the period recorded his songs.

Aníbal Nazaré (1908–75) was a poet, composer and showbiz entrepreneur whose name is strongly associated with a type of Portuguese satirical theatre called *revista*. It was quite common for songs created for *revista* to become very popular Fados, and this happened to a number of his works.

Gabriel de Oliveira (1891–1953), also known as Gabriel Marújo (Gabriel the sailor) due to his years with the Portuguese Navy, was a traditional poet responsible for some of the most popular Fado lyrics. He was born in Rua do Capelão, in Lisbon's Mouraria district, traditionally the epicentre of Fado.

Alexandre O'Neill (1924–86) was a highly acclaimed poet and founder member of the surrealist movement in Portugal. His work was characterised by playfulness, black humour, parody and an attitude of revolt – indeed he was arrested by the secret police on several occasions – and betrayed a love/hate relationship with his country.

Maria do Rosário Pedreira (b. 1959) is a poet, novelist, translator and currently editor at QuidNovi. As with Fernando Pinto do Amaral and Nuno Júdice, Pedreira has been challenged by the Fado singer Carlos do Carmo to write for Fado, helping to create a bridge between tradition and modernity in the twenty-first century.

José Régio (1901–69) was a Portuguese writer who graduated from Coimbra University with a thesis titled *Trends and Individualities in Portuguese Modern Poetry*. He later co-founded the magazine *Presença*, which would come to be the cornerstone of the second modernist movement in Portugal, and he was a regular contributor to some of the leading Portuguese newspapers of the time.

Henrique Rêgo (1896–1963) was a civil servant who worked for the Portuguese Ministry of War. He used to sing Fado in his youth but became well known as a result of his vast repertoire of lyrics, usually on romantic or bucolic themes. He wrote most of the lyrics for the most important Fados composed and sung by Alfredo Marceneiro.

Alberto Rodrigues (?–1961) was a mid-twentieth century Fado poet. During the 1950s, he owned A Parreirinha de Alfama, a restaurant which remains closely associated with the Fado scene and is currently owned by veteran *fadista* Argentina Santos, who still sings there and in the old days used to double up as the cook.

Amália Rodrigues (1920–99) is the most celebrated singer in the history of Fado. She was originally a peasant who left school at a very young age, but through composer Alain Oulman's influence she adopted the poetry of the greatest Portuguese writers, both classic and contemporary, and later in life also wrote some of her own lyrics.

Guilherme Pereira da Rosa (1915–91) was a poet and journalist who became director of *O Século*, an established Portuguese broadsheet owned by the Pereira da Rosa family. As a poet, he had a very productive relationship with some of the main singers of Fado's golden era and a number of his poems were turned into Fado classics by key *fadistas* such as Alfredo Marceneiro.

Augusto de Sousa (?–1972) was a poet whose lyrics were made popular by the great Alfredo Marceneiro. He was active in the 1930s, 40s and 50s, and his best-known lyric was 'Amor é Água que Corre', set to music by Alfredo Marceneiro and still sung by many Fado singers of the younger generation.

Júlio de Sousa (1906–66) was a multi-talented artist who graduated in fine arts and worked as a book illustrator, stage set designer, painter and sculptor. He published several poetry collections and enjoyed giving readings. His poems were particularly compatible with Fado Canção (see p. 13) and for a number of years he ran a Fado house in the Bairro Alto district of Lisbon where he used to read his poetry accompanied by the piano.

José Carlos Ary dos Santos (1936–84) was a precocious talent who began writing at the age of fourteen and was a published author by the time he was sixteen. Born into a bourgeois family, he later joined the Communist Party and was openly gay. He became one of the most familiar names in Portuguese popular poetry of the twentieth century and his artistic association with singer Carlos do Carmo played an important role in the rehabilitation of Fado in the period just after the 1974 revolution.

Amadeu do Vale (1898–1963) was a poet and author of some 200 plays, both originals and adaptations. Some of his poems, like 'Ai! Mouraria', became Fado classics sung by the most important *fadistas* of his era.

ENGLISH LANGUAGE POETS

Moniza Alvi (b. 1954) was born in Pakistan and grew up in Hertfordshire. She has published six collections of poetry including *The Country at My Shoulder* (OUP, 1993) and *Europa* (Bloodaxe Books, 2008). In 2002 she received a Cholmondeley Award from the Society of Authors. Currently she is working on versions of the French poet Jules Supervielle. She tutors for the Poetry School.

Judith Barrington (b. 1944) has published three collections of poetry, most recently the award-winning *Horses and the Human Soul* (Story Line Press, 2004). She has also translated poetry by Cristina Peri Rossi. Among her awards are the Dulwich Festival International Poetry Prize and the Stuart Holbrook Award from Literary Arts. She is a faculty member of the University of Alaska's MFA Program. http://www.judithbarrington.com

David Constantine's (b. 1944) most recent publications are: poems, *Nine Fathom Deep* (Bloodaxe Books, 2009), and short stories, *The Shieling* (Comma Press, 2009). He is a translator of Hölderlin, Kleist, Brecht and Goethe. His translation of Goethe's *Faust* was published by Penguin in 2005 and 2009. With his wife Helen he edits *Modern Poetry in Translation*.

Alfred Corn (b. 1943) is the author of nine books of poems, the most recent titled *Contradictions* (Copper Canyon Press, 2002). In 2008 the University of Michigan Press published *Atlas: Selected Essays, 1989-2007*. A new edition of *The Poem's Heartbeat*, his study of prosody, is published by Copper Canyon (2008). Fellowships include the Guggenheim, the NEA, an Award in Literature from the Academy of Arts and Letters, and one from the Academy of American Poets. He spends half of every year in the UK.

Ruth Fainlight's (b. 1931) *New & Collected Poems* will be published by Bloodaxe Books in late 2010, and her translation of *Sophocles' Theban Plays*, in collaboration with the classicist Robert Littman, came out in 2009 from Johns Hopkins University Press. She has translated poetry by Spanish, Latin-American and Portuguese poets (most notably Sophia de Mello Breyner), and books of her poems have appeared in French, Spanish, Portuguese, Italian and Romanian translation.

Elaine Feinstein (b. 1930) is an acclaimed poet, novelist and translator. She has a Cholmondeley Award for Poetry, and her *Collected Poems and Translations* (Carcanet, 2002) was a Poetry Book Society Special Commendation. Her versions of the poems of Marina Tsvetaeva have received three translation awards from Arts Council, England. She has been a Fellow of the Royal Society of Literature since 1981 and is now serving on its Council. She has written fourteen novels, many radio plays, television dramas, and five biographies, including *Ted Hughes: The Life of a Poet* (Weidenfeld and Nicholson, 2001)

Grey Gowrie (b. 1939) was born in Dublin. He has taught literature at Harvard and University College London and served as Minister for the Arts in the British Government as well as Provost of the Royal College of Arts. His *Third Day: New and Selected Poems* (Carcanet, 2008) was a Poetry Book Society Recommendation.

Marilyn Hacker (b. 1942) has published many collections, including works of poetry, criticism and translation, most recently *NAMES* (W.W. Norton, 2009). She has received numerous honours, including the National Book Award, the Lambda Literary Award, the John Masefield Memorial Award of the Poetry Society of America, and the PEN Award for Poetry in Translation. In 2008, she was elected a Chancellor of the Academy of American Poets. She lives in New York City and Paris.

Philip Jenkins (b. 1959) is a poet and translator of poetry written in Spanish and Portuguese. *Still Life with Loops*, his selection and translation of the Spanish poetry of Eli Tolaretxipi, was published in Arc Publications' *Visible Poets* series in 2008. He has translated a number of poems by other Spanish and Portuguese-language poets, including the Brazilian poet Felipe Fortuna. He lives in Salamanca, Spain.

Fady Joudah's (b. 1971) first poetry collection, *The Earth in the Attic* (Yale University Press, 2008), won the Yale Series for Younger Poets award. He is also the acclaimed translator of Mahmoud

Darwish's poetry, *The Butterfly's Burden* (Bloodaxe Books, 2007) and *If I Were Another* (Farrar Straus Giroux, 2009).

Sarah Maguire (b. 1957) has published four, highly-acclaimed volumes of poetry, the most recent of which, *The Pomegranates of Kandahar* (Chatto & Windus, 2007), was short-listed for the 2007 T.S. Eliot Prize. Founder and Director of The Poetry Translation Centre, her translations of the Sudanese poet, Al-Saddiq Al-Raddi and the Afghan poet, Partaw Naderi, were published in 2008. Collections of her poems are published in Arabic, Norwegian and Malayalam.

Eric Ormsby (b. 1941) has published six collections of poetry, including *For a Modest God* (Grove Press, 1997) and, most recently, *Time's Covenant* (Biblioasis, 2007). His poems have appeared in *The New Yorker, Paris Review,* and *PN Review,* and are included in *The Norton Anthology of Poetry*. Carcanet will publish a new selection of his poems in 2011.

Don Paterson (b. 1963) lives in Dundee, works as an editor and musician, and teaches poetry at the University of St Andrews. His most recent collections include *Landing Light* (Faber, 2004), *Orpheus* (Faber, 2006), a version of Rilke's *Die Sonette an Orpheus,* and *Rain* (Faber, 2009). He is currently working on a book about Shakespeare's sonnets.

Pascale Petit's (b. 1953) latest collection is *What the Water Gave Me: Poems after Frida Kahlo* (Seren, 2010). She has published five collections, two of which were shortlisted for the T.S. Eliot Prize and chosen as Books of the Year in the *TLS* and *The Independent*. The Poetry Book Society selected her as a Next Generation Poet. She tutors poetry courses at Tate Modern. Her website is http://www.pascalepetit.co.uk.

Carol Rumens's (b. 1944) poetry collections include *Poems, 1968-2004* (Bloodaxe Books, 2004), *Blind Spots* (Seren, 2008) and *De Chirico's Threads* (Seren, 2010). She has published occasional fiction, including a novel, *Plato Park* (Chatto, 1987). Her translations of Russian poets (Pushkin, Yevgeny Rein, Kudriavitsky, Ratushinskata, etc.) appear in various anthologies, and her own poems are translated into Polish, Romanian and Russian.

Fiona Sampson (b. 1968) has published seventeen books, most recently *Rough Music* (Carcanet, 2010), *Poetry Writing* (Robert Hale, 2009) and *A Century of Poetry Review* (Carcanet, 2009), a Poetry Book Society Special Commendation, with ten in translation. She has been awarded the Newdigate Prize, been short-listed for Forward single-poem and T.S. Eliot prizes and received a Cholmondeley Award. Forthcoming are the Newcastle/Bloodaxe Poetry Lectures and the Faber Poet-to-poet *Shelley*.

Michael Schmidt (b. 1947) is Professor of Poetry at the University of Glasgow. He is editorial director of Carcanet Press and general editor of *PN Review*. He is a critic and literary historian. His *Collected Poems* were published by Smith/Doorstop in 2009.

George Szirtes (b. 1948) was born in Budapest and came to England as a refugee in 1956. He trained as a painter in Leeds and London, and is the author of a number of acclaimed poetry collections, including *Reel* (Bloodaxe, 2004) which won the T S Eliot prize. He is a Fellow of the Royal Society of Literature and has also written plays, musicals, opera libretti and oratorios, books for children, art criticism and many award-winning works of translation. His own work has been widely translated.

MIMI KHALVATI

Mimi Khalvati has published six poetry collections with Carcanet Press. Her most recent book, *The Meanest Flower*, was a Poetry Book Society Recommendation and was shortlisted for the T.S. Eliot Prize 2007. She is the founder of The Poetry School and co-editor of its anthologies of new writing published by Enitharmon Press. She has received a Cholmondeley Award from the Society of Authors and is a Fellow of the Royal Society of Literature.

RUI VIEIRA NERY

Rui Vieira Nery is a distinguished musicologist who has worked at the Calouste Gulbenkian Foundation in Lisbon since 1982. His research interests include cross-cultural genres in Portuguese music, from sixteenth-century Villancico to contemporary Fado. In 1985, he joined the Department of Musical Sciences of the Lisbon Universidade Nova and became Associate Professor of the Department of Arts at the University of Évora in 2000. He has also served as the Secretary of State for Culture in the Portuguese Government (1995–97). He has published many articles and a number of musicological studies, two of which received the Musicology Award of the Portuguese National Music Council.